The Biblical Integration of FAMILY, WORK & MINISTRY

A FATHER'S STEW

Stephen Beck

NEW YORK

A FATHER'S STEW

The Biblical Integration of FAMILY, WORK & MINISTRY

Stephen Beck

Copyright ©2006 Stephen Beck

ISBN: 1-60037-117-5 (Hardcover)

ISBN: 1-933596-54-6 (Paperback)

ISBN: 1-60037-119-1 (Audio)

ISBN: 1-60037-118-3 (eBook)

Published by:

MORGAN · JAMES
THE ENTREPRENEURIAL PUBLISHER

Morgan James Publishing, LLC
1225 Franklin Ave Ste 325
Garden City, NY 11530-1693
Toll Free 800-485-4943
www.MorganJamesPublishing.com

Interior Design by:
Heather Kirk
www.BrandedForSuccess.com
Heather@BrandedForSuccess.com

Habitat
for Humanity®
Peninsula
Building Partner

 **DEDICATION**

For my father, James Doughty Beck III — the consummate gentleman, who in the last hours of wakefulness, was reconciled to the One to Whom we must all give an account.

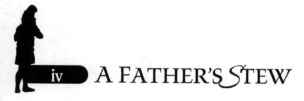

# RAVE REVIEWS

"Every young couple should read this book!"

~Laurie Bluedorn Teaching the Trivium

"In *A Father's Stew*, Steve Beck mines Scripture to paint a biblical picture of our life — that God-pleasing aroma of Christ — as a stew: a mixture of family, work and ministry. Mr. Beck's humble, down-to-earth language of this heavenly plan has challenged me to deny the worldly tendency to view my life as a TV dinner, where every aspect of my life is a separate compartment to be walled off and shut down as I move into another area. God never meant it to be that way, and my life is really a stew: a mixture of responsibilities, faithfulness and obedience that when balanced, blend together to create a pleasing sacrifice to God."

~Jim Bob Howard, Highlands Study Center

"The book is EXCELLENT! Direct, biblical, meaty, but yet simple and without condemnation. Wow! I can hardly wait to see what else you've written."

~Debbie Cariker, The Eclectic Homeschool Online

"If the book, *A Father's Stew* is an example of your efforts, all I can say is 'keep up the good work'!! Thank you."

~Rose Freeman

"Stephen Beck doesn't just write about what it means for a father to lead his family — he's lived the life. And drawing from his experiences, he makes a passionate appeal for other men to take the steps necessary to better guide and serve their family."

~Wesley Strackbein, The Vision Forum

"*A Father's Stew* arrived Tuesday night, and my husband started reading it right away. Thank you for allowing the Lord to work through you both. I know this is a huge issue with many home-schooling Fathers. Thank you again for your willingness to submit and be used by God. God Bless You."

~Michelle

"...grab your Bible and your highlighter, and plan to spend some time on your knees — or on your face — before a Holy God when you read this heart grabber. Yet, don't think this is some femi-Nazi book designed to condemn men, or a book written from a 'holier-than-thou' perspective. This will encourage you to obey the Word, live for God, and disciple your children. Beck uses his own life and the lives of well-known Bible men to first commiserate, and then point you to the right path. Hey, guys; this is do-able!"

~From Eclectic Homeschool Online (for complete review)

vi A FATHER'S STEW

TABLE OF CONTENTS

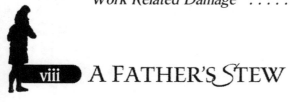

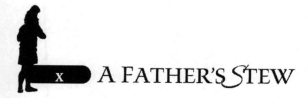
A FATHER'S STEW

ACKNOWLEDGEMENTS

I am very grateful to Kevin Smith for editing this manuscript — if you ever get bored with flying jets, you would make a great editor!

I am grateful to Janell Robertson for making the "ready for printing" side of this project so easy.

Most of all, I am grateful to my wife, Kerry, for being my partner in the molding of those we will leave behind.

A FATHER'S STEW

 **PREFACE**

The Bible states that without a vision, the people perish. I have a dream, a vision if you will. In my dream, I wake up excited to start another day at work. Surely, you must be dreaming you say! No, I am excited because I know that this work is the very work that God has called me to do.

My wife is my right hand in this work and I know that God could not have given me anyone better suited to this task. My children are involved in my work and it proves to be a tremendous training ground for them. For my daughters, as they submit to me and follow my leadership, I am able to train them to be godly wives and mothers someday. For my son, I am able to teach him to obey God and one day, lead a family of his own. Younger men are also involved in my work and working side by side gives me the opportunity to teach them to apply God's Word with wisdom and understanding in their daily affairs. My wife ministers to younger women as well, teaching them to honor their husbands and love their children in a godly manner.

My children see these young men and women grow and are encouraged to one day disciple younger believers on their own. The younger men and women see my children and realize that the Bible is true and a godly family can be achieved. My work blesses my family and my ministry. My family helps me in my work and provides concrete examples for my ministry. My ministry provides helpers for my work and motivation for my family. For you see, work, family and ministry are all ingredients to a stew. A stew that is described in Phil 4:18 as a sweet-smelling aroma, an acceptable sacrifice, well pleasing to God.

INTRODUCTION

At first glance, this book may seem like a random odyssey winding its way through the complicated subjects of family, ministry and work. Is this guy a nut tackling three subjects that could each make for a very long book? How can he possibly do justice to the three areas that seem to touch every waking moment of our lives and still end up with a relatively short book?

Simple. The basic issue in all three of these areas is **obedience to the Word of God.**

Actually, balancing and integrating our family, ministry and work is a biblical concept. Look at the model woman of Proverbs 31. She provides food and clothing for her family. She ministers to the poor. She even considers a field and plants a vineyard with the profits from a home-based business. Yet, she does all this in a way that pleases God. All of her endeavors work in harmony and do not rob from one another. She has identified God's priorities and oriented her life to line up with those priorities. Unfortunately, some have pointed to this woman as a model for Christian feminism.

Yet, her family remains the object of all her hard work. This should dispel the notion that God rewards women who put their careers over their home life.

Consider Job. Here was a man who was also able to integrate his family, ministry and work. The Bible describes him as blameless and upright. His children were a blessing to him, his wife and one another. His adult children ate meals together and had fellowship in one another's houses. Evidence of his high priority on family is demonstrated by the fact that he prayed for his adult children and regularly made sacrifices for them lest they had erred against God (Job 1:4-5). He ministered to the poor and the fatherless. He provided for the widows and stood against evil (Job 29:12-17). Job's uprightness also flowed into his business dealings. He ran a very large ranch and provided for his many servants. He was considered a very influential man (Job 1:3), running his business with integrity (Job 31:5-6) and treating his servants with respect (Job 31:13-15). In short, Job was a man who, through obedience, was able to glorify God by successfully integrating family, ministry and work without causing these areas to compete against and destroy one another.

But excelling in our families, ministries and work is no easy task. Many a man has disqualified himself for ministry by having ungodly children (1 Timothy 3:4-5). Even more men have sacrificed their children in the pursuit of their careers. Some have even sacrificed their families in pursuit of ministry. What is the path of righteousness in these three

A FATHER'S STEW

areas? How can we please God in the areas of family, ministry and work? How can we balance these three areas so that our God and King is glorified? I would submit that the common thread woven throughout the tremendous problems we see today in our families, ministries and work is found in the twelfth chapter of Romans:

> And do not be conformed to this world, but be transformed by the renewing of your mind, that you may prove what is that good and acceptable and perfect will of God. *(Romans 12:2)*

Paul is commanding us **not** to be shaped by the prevailing culture. Instead, we are to be transformed by a different culture — a Christian culture. And what is this Christian culture based on? The Word of God.

Notice that obedience to this verse is a two-fold process. We are to reject the ungodly culture around us **while at the same time** allowing God to transform our lives by embracing the godly culture found in His Word. Without **doing both at the same time**, we can fall into one of two traps.

THE TRAP OF ASCETICISM

If we only reject the current culture and are not transformed by the Word of God, we slip into asceticism; trying to achieve righteousness by "touch not, taste not, handle not".

Therefore, if you died with Christ from the basic principles of the world, why, as though living in the world, do you subject yourselves to regulations — "Do not touch, do not taste, do not handle," which all concern things which perish with the using — according to the commandments and doctrines of men? **These things indeed have an appearance of wisdom** in self-imposed religion, false humility, and neglect of the body, **but are of no value against the indulgence of the flesh**. *(Col 2:20-23)*

Rejecting the current culture without the renewal of our minds will result in the **appearance** of righteousness, but the end result will be unsuccessful. Why? Because "in you (that is, in your flesh), dwells no good thing" (Romans 7:18) and our hearts are "deceitful above all things and desperately wicked (Jeremiah 17:9)."

This idea of the "appearance of righteousness" can run in two directions. The unbeliever can deceive himself by doing "good works" in order to achieve righteousness before God. He may go to church, give to charities, love his family or even be a leader in the community, but all of these activities do not address the fundamental problem between God and man. Paul made this point to the Romans:

A FATHER'S STEW

For if Abraham was justified by works, he has something to boast about, **but not before God**. For what does the Scripture say? "Abraham believed God, and it was accounted to him for righteousness." Now to him who works, the wages are not counted as grace but as debt. But to him who does not work but believes on Him **who justifies the ungodly**, his faith is accounted for righteousness, just as David also describes the blessedness of the man to whom God imputes righteousness apart from works: *(Romans 4:2-6)*

If you work for an employer, he owes you a wage at the end of the day. But what if you owed that employer a debt so great that it could never be repaid — even if you worked every day for the rest of your life? It would be silly to demand right standing (or balanced books) with your employer for a few days work when you owed so great a debt! Similarly, it is silly for us to demand right standing before a holy God on account of a few "good" things we have done, when our sin has caused a debt too great to repay. Read the above verse again. God extends forgiveness of this debt to those who first realize they are ungodly, and then believe in "Him who justifies the ungodly". Jesus Christ died on the cross to pay the debt for which we were rightfully liable (Romans 5:8). We can never repay that debt through our "good" deeds and in fact, it is strictly prohibited. For God imputes righteousness apart from works. This idea is echoed in Ephesians.

> For by grace you have been saved through faith, and that **not of yourselves**; it is the gift of God, **not of works**, lest anyone should boast. *(Ephesians 2:8-9)*

Jesus saved His harshest words for those who were trying to earn their own righteousness before God by rejecting the current culture. The Pharisees had the rejection of their surrounding culture down to a science, but without saving faith in the only begotten Son of God, it proved to be worthless. He called them "white-washed sepulchers" who were clean on the outside, but were full of rot and decay on the inside.

But this "appearance of righteousness" can run in another direction as well. **Believers** can reject the things in our culture that the Bible requires them to. However, without the transformation of our minds by the Word of God, we can achieve the "appearance" of righteousness without the **power**. One of the greatest dangers of our modern evangelical church is the "hired gun" syndrome. We hire pastors, along with scads of assistant pastors, and expect them to fight the battle for us. We have become a generation of "evan-jelly fish" as Douglas Wilson aptly puts it. Christians without a theological backbone. The Word of God gives us the backbone necessary to fight the prevailing

culture. Rejection of the current culture without the transforming power of the Word of God in our lives leaves only the shadow of true spirituality.

THE TRAP OF LICENTIOUSNESS

Although we are to avoid the first trap of rejecting our current culture without the attending transformation, most modern evangelical Christians fall into a second trap. We try to be transformed by the Word of God without rejecting anything our society places in front of us. We want all of what God has for us...and everything the world has as well. We attend church, listen to Christian tapes, listen to Christian music, attend Christian conferences, throw ourselves in Bible studies and yet our families, ministries and work look surprisingly similar to that of the world. We are like the women in Second Timothy who are "always learning, but never able to come to the knowledge of the truth." In fact, Paul said these women were loaded down with sins and led away by their lusts. Does this sound familiar? How can we expect transformation when we are also are loaded down with sins and led away by our lusts?

One of the most common complaints among Christian men today is that of frustration. We truly want to please God in our family, ministry and work, but our lives seem to fall so short. What little Christian fruit we bear is choked out by the world's thorns and thistles. We are not to be conformed to this world. In addition to the transforming of our hearts and minds by God, we must also reject society's constant pressure to swallow ideas that run contrary to the Word of God. We must reject the notion that:

- There are many paths to righteousness before God apart from His Son.

- We are free to make decisions apart from Scripture.

- There are areas in our lives that Scripture has not addressed.

- God does not care what we do behind closed doors.

- Women must enter the work force in order to be "truly" fulfilled.

- Our children must be educated by so-called "experts" — that when God gave us children, He did not give us all of the resources necessary to fully educate them.

- We can place our children in concentration camps euphemistically called child-care centers while we pursue our careers, hobbies and bank accounts.

- We can tolerate sexual sin in our churches and not be judged by God.

- We can live as if God's number one priority is our own happiness.

Basically, we are to reject the notion that we, as Christians, can have it all! Our job, as believers, is to identify and reject the sinful practices and ideas of this current

A FATHER'S STEW

culture **while at the same time**, being transformed by a different culture. We are to be transformed by the Christian culture found in the Word of God. With this charge in mind, let us look at the first step toward successfully integrating our family, work and ministry.

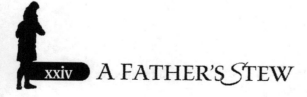

A FATHER'S STEW

First Things First

SECTION 1

2 A FATHER'S STEW

CHAPTER 1

THE WORD OF GOD

THE SUFFICIENCY OF SCRIPTURE

Preparing a dish from scratch is no easy task, even with a recipe. Being a genuine cooking novice myself, I can readily attest to this. I spend so much time trying to figure out terms such as "folding," "browning," and "braising," that I can never get to the actual cooking part! In godly living, as well as cooking, there are some basic principles and premises we must first understand before we can even begin. The first and foremost premise is the **sufficiency of Scripture**. Second Timothy 3:16 and 17 states:

> All Scripture is given by inspiration of God, and is profitable for doctrine, for reproof, for correction, for instruction in righteousness, **that the man of God may be complete, thoroughly equipped for every good work**.

Scripture thoroughly equips us to live a godly life. There is nothing else we need to be complete. Do you believe that?

Do you believe that you could read only one book all your life and still be a complete (mature) man or woman of God? All decisions in our lives are addressed either directly or indirectly by God's Word. I say directly or indirectly because the Bible teaches us according to precepts and principles. Precepts are expressed commandments given from Scripture and principles are conclusions drawn from those precepts. For example, the Bible commands us to love our wives as Christ loved the church. The commandment is simple enough, but the way in which we do this takes some studying. How did Christ love the church? He taught her the Word. He praised her when she did well and rebuked her when she needed it (Revelation 2:1-6). He sacrificed everything to achieve her best interest. Although the **precepts** of God seem to be limited to specific behaviors and situations, the **principles** derived from those precepts transcend all situations and cultures.

A warning is warranted, however. Although we are to obey the Word fully and in its entirety, we are not to add to the Word of God. The Bible prohibits drunkenness in Ephesians 5:18, but it does not prohibit the drinking of alcohol. Paul did not exhort Timothy to drink a little grape juice for his stomach ailment (1 Timothy 5:23) and Jesus most certainly did not change the water into some unfermented fruit drink at the wedding in Cana. However we may feel about the consumption of alcohol, we are not allowed to place more restrictions than the Word of God does. Spurgeon, once said in regards to tobacco smoking that he found it hard enough to obey the ten commandments and had no intention of adding an eleventh!

It is amazing how we want to ignore **obvious** commands found in Scripture, while at the same time, try to add commands where God has not. Why do we do this? Because **we** want to be the final arbiter over God's Word. We want to be like the Most High. There is no reward for being "holier" than God in a certain area. In fact, instead of a reward, you may receive a rebuke. My point is **not** to encourage believers to use their freedom in Christ towards licentiousness. My point is to demonstrate that in God's economy, there is for no room for intellectually lazy Christians. We are to show ourselves approved, rightly dividing the Word of Truth (2 Timothy 2:15). The One to Whom we will all give an account, has commanded us to become mature in our understanding of His Word (1 Corinthians 14:20).

So we see that Scripture is sufficient to rule **all** areas of our lives. Scripture is the ultimate authority to which we must look. If we want to know what our families should look like, we should go to the Scriptures. If we want to know how our children should be educated, we should go to the Scriptures. If we want to know what kind of ministry we should be involved in, we should go to the Scriptures. If we want to know want career to pursue we should, you guessed it, go to the Scriptures. One of the reasons we fail so miserably at balancing family, ministry and work is that we do not know what God's Word says about these areas.

OUR CULTURE IGNORES SCRIPTURE

Our current culture and even the modern evangelical church is very reminiscent of the days of Josiah (2 Chronicles 34:14-21). God's Word had been lost for many years and was suddenly found when repairs were being made to the temple. When the priest read God's Word to Josiah, he was cut to the quick and realized that he had not "kept the Word of the Lord, to do according to all that is written in this book." Can you imagine? God's people without God's Word for generations! How would they know what to do? How would they know if they were pleasing God? The fact is, they did not. Without the Word of God as the standard of measurement for all things, we inevitably fail to please God — no matter how hard we try or how sincere our hearts. Although Josiah had been a good king up to this point, he realized that God must be served according to **His** prescribed manner. When confronted with the truth, he repented and did it God's way. We, on the other hand, have even less excuse because we have God's Word at our finger tips and yet we fail to apply His standard to every area of our lives. We fail to see the sufficiency of Scripture for every decision we make.

Do you truly believe that the Bible holds all the information necessary to make you a complete person? Are you willing to do anything it takes to obey God's Word? Are you willing to be transformed by the renewing of your mind, that you may prove what is that good and acceptable and perfect will of God (Romans 12:2)? Then it is time to take the "sneaker" test!

A FATHER'S STEW

I heard of the sneaker test on a tape from Douglas Phillips. If a man came to you and said, "Sir, I see that you are wearing sneakers. Now you know that sneakers are an abomination to the Lord and I am rebuking you in the name of the Lord Jesus Christ to take off those sneakers and repent right away!" Well, we could give one of several answers. We could tell the man he is crazy. We could ignore him. Or we could say something like this. "Sir, I have never heard that the Lord abhors sneakers, but if you can demonstrate to me biblically that this is true...in the trash they will go, you will never find me or my family wearing sneakers again!"

Do you have that attitude toward the Word of God? Could there be things in the Scriptures that God has not revealed to you yet? When He does reveal them to you, will you be willing to obey them? Mark Twain once said, "It's not the parts of the Bible that I don't understand that bother me, it is the parts that I do!"

NO SUBSTITUTIONS, PLEASE

Scripture is the final authority on what God wants us to do and the way He wants us to do it. This was brought home to me in a big way when my college roommates decided to make lasagna. After mixing the ground meat and ricotta cheese, they realized they were missing the lasagna noodles (For the culinary challenged — those long flat ones you put on the top and bottom). Of course being men, they knew how to improvise. When they set the "lasagna" on the table, I stared in disbelief and asked what in the world they had done. They stated with pride that since they were missing the lasagna noodles, they had substituted with the next best thing they could find in the freezer — a bag of frozen tater-tots! Although their hearts were in the right place, and they had worked very hard, they succeeded in making "lasagna" that even the dog would not eat!

We are like those college roommates when we try to substitute our ideas for those found in His Word. Unless we use God-ordained ingredients to make our "stew," we will inevitably make something that is not pleasing to God. It is not enough to try our best to please God in our families, work and ministry. **God does not bless us for trying hard.** If He blessed for sincerity and hard work, the cults who deny the deity of Christ would win hands down! God only blesses those decisions that are in accordance with Scripture. **Let me say that again, God only blesses decisions that are biblical!** And what constitutes a biblical decision is not open to private interpretation. A decision is either based on the expressed Word of God (or a principle derived from the expressed Word of God) or it is not. This is why we are required to know the whole counsel of God (Acts 20:27).

NO PRIVATE INTERPRETATIONS

God's Word is not open to private interpretation (2 Peter 1:20-21). One of the greatest dangers in our modern "Christian" culture is the focus on ourselves.

A FATHER'S STEW

"What does this passage mean to me personally?"

"God has different priorities for me than He does for you."

"My God is a God of love and would never send anyone to Hell."

"I don't believe in the doctrine of election. It doesn't seem fair to me."

"God did not mean a literal "day" when He said He created the world in six days (Even though He said morning and evening after each day and even stated which number of day it was!). Besides, I would feel stupid believing such a simple explanation."

The problem with looking through this myopic lens is that God's Word becomes very subjective. If I interpret the Bible this way and you interpret the Bible another way, then which interpretation is correct? Can we really know what the Bible is saying if there are so many different ways of interpreting it? Is there really such a thing as absolute truth? When we view Scripture as applying to each of us differently, we are thinking as a humanist. We are placing ourselves as the final arbiter over God's Word. I determine what God means in this passage for me, and you determine what this passage means for you. God knew exactly what He meant when He wrote the Bible and it is our responsibility, through the Holy Spirit, to understand what He meant and to conform our lives to His Word.

When we try to change the plain meaning of the Scriptures to fit our current culture, we are assuming the role of God. Allowing women to teach men in the church is a good example of this. 1 Timothy 2:11-15 clearly teaches against this and yet many of our modern evangelical churches have women teaching men in adult Sunday schools. The Bible does not allow a woman to teach a man even if she has a male teaching partner. It makes no difference if those being taught are couples, either. Women are not to be in authority over men in the church, period. God's Word is not open to our higher criticism. We are not allowed to say, "Well I know that God's Word says this, but what He **really** meant was..." Instead of asking what God's Word means in this day and time, ask what has God's Word meant throughout the ages and determine to understand it and then obey it! Your truth alarm should always go off when you read something that claims to be a "new" principle or "secret to living the Christian life."

NO SELECTIVE OBEDIENCE

So far we have seen that Scripture is sufficient for all our decisions, we can not substitute man's wisdom for God's Word and the Bible is not open to private interpretation. There is one more concept we must acknowledge to allow the Bible to have its full impact in our lives. In 1 Samuel

A FATHER'S STEW

15:3, Saul was instructed by God to attack the Amalekites and to not spare any man, woman, child or animal. God was executing His divine judgment on them, which He had a perfect right to do (1 Samuel 15:2). Saul attacked the Amalekites, but he spared the king and the best of the animals. When confronted by Samuel, Saul claimed that the animals had been spared to sacrifice to God. Samuel wasn't fooled for a moment.

> Then Samuel said: "Has the LORD as great delight in burnt offerings and sacrifices, as in obeying the voice of the LORD? **Behold, to obey is better than sacrifice**, and to heed than the fat of rams. For rebellion is as the sin of witchcraft, and stubbornness is as iniquity and idolatry. Because you have rejected the word of the LORD, he also has rejected you from being king." *(1 Samuel 15:22-23)*

God's Word must be obeyed God's way. No amount of church attendance, giving, Bible study, evangelism, prayer or good works can make up for disobedience to the Word of God. Notice how subtle Saul's argument was. He only spared King Agag because he wanted to show mercy. God wants us to show mercy, right? He only spared the animals so he could sacrifice them to God. God commands sacrifices, does He not?

Earlier, Saul offered a burnt offering to the Lord (which only the priests were allowed to do) and explained his disobedience by claiming that he wanted God's blessing on the coming battle. God wants to bless us, correct? God's commands must be obeyed God's way. Disobedience is rebellion and rebellion is the same as the sin of witchcraft (1 Samuel 15:22-23). When we disobey the Word of God, we are rejecting it and God will reject us from serving Him. James put it another way.

> If any of you lacks wisdom, let him ask of God, who gives to all liberally and without reproach, and it will be given to him. But let him ask in faith, with no doubting, for he who doubts is like a wave of the sea driven and tossed by the wind. For let not that man suppose that he will receive anything from the Lord; he is a double-minded man, unstable in all his ways. *(James 1:5-8)*

What a great promise! If we want to know God's thoughts, if we want wisdom from the Creator of the universe, if we want to choose between better and best — God will give us the answer! But this promise comes with a condition. We must be willing to obey whatever He commands us. We do not have the right to pick and choose His commandments like items on a salad bar.

"I like this command, but that one seems too old fashioned."

"I know adultery is a sin, but monogamous homosexuality is surely not."

"I believe the Bible, but I would rather not spank my child."

"I like what Jesus teaches, but Paul is too harsh, especially in regards to women."

"I know this believer is having an affair, but how can we minister to him if we break fellowship with him?"

We have no right to all of the information at hand before we decide to obey. Eve thought she needed just a little more information before she obeyed. She got her wish — the knowledge of good and evil! When faced with a command or principle found in Scripture, we do not have the right to debate whether our option or God's option is better. We are to ask in faith. The faith that, whatever a loving God would instruct us to do, will be for our ultimate good (Romans 8:28).

We are not to doubt God's goodness. We are not to weigh our options. If we come to God with this attitude, James states we should expect **nothing** in return. How many times have your children asked your advice, only to ignore it when the time came for action? About the third or fourth time you quit giving advice and let them learn for themselves — the hard way! Or at least I hope you would. But alas, another of our modern evangelical failings is that of disciplining our children **according to the Bible**. If you hate your children then do not discipline them (Proverbs 13:24). And if you really hate your children, never spank them (Proverbs 23:13-14). Sons, whose mothers bail them out of trouble over and over, will marry wives who will be forced to do the same thing — or at least until the divorce papers are signed. Remember, God's rules must be obeyed God's way!

A FATHER'S STEW

GODLY PRIORITIES

CHAPTER 2

DOES GOD HAVE PRIORITIES?

Although we are required by Scripture to know the whole counsel of God (Acts 20:27), we would be foolish to not identify and understand God's top priorities. Are you surprised that God has priorities? Are there actually commandments or principles that take precedence over others in the Bible? Are there some commandments that, if not given top priority, will affect all other decisions downstream? There certainly are and we would do well to identify them and implement them first.

Take the example of elders in 1 Timothy 3:4-5. If a man does not fulfill the **first priority** of ruling his household well (having obedient children and a submissive wife), then he should not even consider (or be considered) for the **subsequent priority** of shepherding the church. God places a higher priority on a godly family than He does on a godly ministry! The Bible makes no distinction between pastors and elders here. A pastor whose household is unruly should step down until the household is brought back to order. This will benefit both the pastor and the ones to whom he is ministering.

In the twelfth chapter of Mark, one of the scribes asked Jesus a very interesting question. He asked our Lord which was the first commandment. Here is a man asking **God** what His highest priorities are. What an insightful man! We would do well to ask God the same question. Of all the things that are written down in the Scriptures, what are the ones not to be missed? The ones that if missed will affect all the other areas of my life. Jesus answered the scribe by saying, "All of the commandments are important. No one commandment is more important than the other." No! Read the **real** answer Christ gave to the scribe.

> Jesus answered him, "The first of all the commandments is: 'Hear, O Israel, the Lord our God, the Lord is one. 'And you shall love the Lord your God with all your heart, with all your soul, with all your mind, and with all your strength.' This is the first commandment. And the second, like it, is this: 'You shall love your neighbor as yourself.' There is no other commandment greater than these." *(Mark 12:29-31)*

Here is the Son of God actually claiming that some commandments take priority over others. There are some commandments, that if not obeyed first, cause all subsequent decisions and good works to be distorted. Why this focus on godly priorities? **If we do not understand what things are most important to God and implement them first, all subsequent decisions will be adversely affected.** To put it another way, if we do not first lay a firm foundation (based on the priorities of God found in His Word), the rest of the building (our lives and those close to us) will be subject to weakness and will eventually collapse. We, as a people of God, have done a very poor job at identifying what things are most important to God. What are the things closest to His heart and in line with His will? Is it no wonder when we, as the modern evangelical church, major on the minor issues and treat lightly or ignore the major ones.

> For I desire mercy and not sacrifice, and the knowledge of God more than burnt offerings. *(Hosea 6:6)*

Was God saying He did not want His people to offer sacrifices to Him? No, He had commanded them to do this as part of their worship. **He was identifying His priorities to them.** Mercy and knowledge were to come **before** sacrifices. Mercy and knowledge placed sacrifices in their proper context. To put it another way, God's people will miss the meaning of the sacrifice if they do not understand Who He is (His holiness and what that requires) and His mercy (the sending of His Son to fulfill the righteous requirement for His holiness). The point is that we, as God's people, must identify God's priorities from His Word and then do whatever it takes to make those our priorities as well.

CONFLICTING PRIORITIES

Without clearly defined priorities, people and organizations become frustrated and engage in activities that are at odds with one another. Our centralized, federal government is full of these. The United States government spends billions of dollars trying to increase farm productivity through the Agricultural Extension Service. It then turns right around, through the PIC program, and pays farmers not to plant because of over-production! Conflicting programs and confusion inevitably result when governments have competing priorities.

Churches have the same problem. Many of our evangelical churches have programs and activities that are at cross purposes with one another and the Word of God. One thing the modern evangelical church has done very poorly is identify God's priorities. Because church leaders do not have a clear understanding of God's priorities, they make decisions that lead them farther and farther away from God's goal of bringing glory to Himself.

Consider the modern church youth group. A church becomes alarmed at the behavior and the lack of scriptural knowledge of their youth. To combat this, they hire a young, hip youth minister. As the kids gravitate toward this young energetic guy, it exacerbates an already widening gap between the children and their parents. The kids begin to view the youth pastor as their spiritual leader instead of the biblical model of their own fathers that we see in Deuteronomy chapter 6. The parents, whom God has called to train their children in His ways, abdicate their responsibility even further because, "Hey, why should I disciple my own kids? That's what our youth pastor gets paid for!" The parents even doubt their **ability** to disciple their kids because they have not been trained to do so. It is the "I am a trained professional, do not attempt this at home" mentality. The demands of the parents and the kids finally become too great for our young youth minister and he departs to start the whole process over again in another church. This leaves the kids in a worse state than before this whole mess started. Although they may have a few tidbits of Scripture in their heads (after all, the youth pastor did have a Wednesday night Bible study!), they have missed a very important principle. The principle of fathers taking the responsibility of discipling their **own** children in the ways of the Lord. These same kids, having missed the principle, will in turn, fail to pass this principle to their own kids, making the same mistake their parents made years before.

You see, decisions made without keeping God's priorities in view will end in disaster and will not accomplish His overall goal — to glorify Himself. Activities not in line with His priorities achieve nothing and can even become counter productive. The modern evangelical church is notorious for being busy in all the lesser things. This siphons precious time, energy and resources away from the most important issues. Programs are instituted to solve problems instead of the biblical model of relationships. If a man is not leading his family well, he does not need a program or a Christian "pep rally" in a football stadium. He needs a mature believer to come alongside to model biblical family leadership. That is why the elders are called to shepherd the flock, not manage the corporation. Church leaders must identify God's priorities and be able to communicate them effectively to a people whose lives are frequently at odds with His priorities. These are the same people who only see the "urgent" need of the moment, not the long-term methodical ascent to Christian maturity through the agency of the Holy Spirit.

Keeping godly priorities in the church is where our theology runs headlong into reality. What things are most important? Where should the church allocate its resources? Is this program addressing only the need of the moment or has it been carefully measured against the over-all goal and priorities of the Word and found to be biblical? Are we acquiescing to personalities in the church? Are we putting our own agenda ahead of God's?

> *"If we don't buy these new hand bells, the choir director will quit."*

> *"I could never take a strong stand on premarital sex from the pulpit, I might offend some and where would they hear the gospel?"*

> *"How can I encourage mothers with small children to quit working a 9-5 job? My kids are in day-care also!"*

A FATHER'S STEW

Every decision must be in light of how it will advance God's ultimate goal of bringing Himself glory and how it adheres to the priorities found in His Word. In order to implement God's priorities, we must first identify them. So let's look at the first great neglected priority of the modern evangelical church.

The First Ingredient: Family

SECTION 2

WHAT DOES
GOD REQUIRE?

THE FIRST GREAT NEGLECTED PRIORITY

From the previous chapter, we understand that Scripture encourages us to identify and then implement the priorities of God. This in turn brings us to the first great neglected priority of the modern evangelical church. When Jesus answered the scribe's question concerning the greatest commandment in Scripture, He quoted from Deuteronomy.

> "Hear, O Israel: The LORD our God, the LORD is one! You shall love the LORD your God with all your heart, with all your soul, and with all your strength. And these words which I command you today shall be in your heart. **You shall teach them diligently to your children, and shall talk of them when you sit in your house, when you walk by the way, when you lie down, and when you rise up**." *(Deuteronomy 6:4-7)*

The greatest commandment in all of Scripture is to love the Lord with all your heart, with all your soul and with all your strength. Yet, how were they to accomplish this? How were they to implement this greatest of all commandments (which, in reality, was a summation of the rest of the commandments as well)? They were to memorize them, obey them and **diligently** teach them to their children! And **when** were they to do this? As they went about their normal activities — when they were at home, when they were away from home, when they were lying down and when they woke up. Basically, they were commanded to instruct their children in godliness **at all times**.

God did not tell His people to teach their children about Him for one hour a week during Sunday school. And when their children reached the age of junior high, He did not tell them to turn the instruction of Him over to a youth pastor. He laid the full responsibility of instructing their children on the **parents** and promised to hold them accountable through blessings and curses. It is the same today. Fathers are to rule their households well, passing the commandments and principles found in the Word of God down to their children who will then be equipped to pass them to their own children. This is God's plan. This is His priority!

Of course, all of this presupposes that parents spend time with their children. How can we train our children in the ways of God during our normal activities if **we are never around them during those normal activities**? How can we give godly instruction in God's prescribed manner if we leave for work before our children wake up and come home after they have gone to bed? Even if we make it home before they go to bed, we must wade through the baseball practice, dinner in shifts (because all everyone in the family has different activities), homework for two hours, baths and finally the last fifteen minutes before bedtime to pass on the godly heritage for which we will be held accountable!

OUR RESPONSIBILITY FOR RAISING GODLY CHILDREN

"But it's not fair to compare our method of raising children with the people of the Old Testament. They had an agrarian society. They had a different culture."

This is where we need to allow the Word of God to over-haul our thinking. This world and its culture is arrayed in battle against us. This world and all of its systems do not have the best interest of your children in mind. In fact, quite the opposite! I believe that one of the greatest curses of our modern work environment is that it separates the fathers from their children for most of the day (and now the mothers when they choose to work). Someone without your convictions about God and without your moral absolutes is having the greater impact on your children by sheer volume of time! Make no mistake, if you are not shaping your child's world view, some one else will be more than happy to do it for you. In fact they will use your tax dollars to do it!

Who is shaping your child's world view? Who is determining your child's culture? But you say, "I send my children to a Christian school" or "We have a great youth pastor at our church". Notice who is responsible to do the training in Deuteronomy 6:7. God will not ask your child's Christian school teacher how they have trained **your** children in righteousness. Nor will He ask the youth pastor for an accounting of **your** children's spiritual instruction. He will point His finger at you, at the judgment seat of Christ, and demand an accounting of the daily training in godliness you gave your children. And what will you say? The job that Thou gavest me, it took away all my time, and I failed to train my children in Your ways. That argument did not work with Adam in the garden concerning Eve and it will not work for you!

> Train up a child in the way he should go,
> and when he is old he will not depart from
> it. *(Proverbs 22:6)*

Many people take the above verse as some sort of vague maxim. "After all, it is a proverb. We all know godly people who have done all they could and still had rebellious kids." I would counter that even if you take this verse only as a proverb, **it should still bear out most of the time.** Is that not the definition of a proverb? But one look at the kids in our evangelical churches today, reveals that we do not consider this even a proverb anymore — much less a promise. We do not expect our kids to be obedient, disciplined and holy. We consider ourselves successful parents if our kids stay away from drugs or refrain from getting pregnant out of wedlock. Correction, most of us consider ourselves successful parents when they come back to the church **after** getting involved in drugs and having sex outside of marriage.

We are not to be conformed to this world. We are to be at war with the existing culture. Make no mistake, even if the Christians do not recognize the war being waged all around them, the world certainly does and is doing it's best to neutralize you and capture your children. Fathers, get in the fight! We are to train our children to not just hunker down and survive in a hostile environment, but to be soldiers who overcome and take captives for the kingdom!

> *"But I don't want to force God down their throat. I want them to come to God on their own. I want it to be their idea."*

What foolishness! Do you have the same attitude regarding algebra? Do you say, "Honey, I don't want to pressure you to learn your algebra. I want it to be your idea. Don't do your work until you are emotionally ready." No! You tell them to go to their room and do their homework — and don't come out until it's done! If we consider algebra something worth teaching and holding our children accountable for, how much more the Word of God! We saw in the sixth chapter of Deuteronomy that we are commanded to diligently teach our children. Later in chapter thirty-two of Deuteronomy we are told:

and He said to them: "Set your hearts on all the words which I testify among you today, which you shall command your children to be careful to observe — all the words of this law. **For it is not a futile thing for you, because it is your life**..." *(Deuteronomy 32:46-47)*

Did you catch that? It is not a futile thing to command our children to obey all of God's Word, because it **is our life!** What is your life's work? Is it your profession? It had better not be! Your life's work as a father must be training up godly children who will in turn be able to train up their own godly children. Look at the verse again. We are to **command** our children to be careful to observe (obey) God's Word. God commands you to teach your children His ways. The only thing you will accomplish by being weak in this endeavor is to give them obstacles they will have to overcome for years.

Some of you may have grown up in homes that stressed obedience, but lacked the love. I am not advocating that. We are to love our children as our heavenly Father loved His own Son. No one has loved His Son more than the Father has and yet, He required obedience from His Son, even to the point of death on a cross. He has also shown no greater love towards us than to send His Son to die on our behalf. Yet, **He still demands our obedience** with a godly fear.

A FATHER'S STEW

He who has My commandments and keeps them, it is he who loves Me. And he who loves Me will be loved by My Father, and I will love him and manifest Myself to him.   *(John 14:21)*

Obedience is the outward manifestation of our love for God. If you say you love God, then obey Him. If someone claims to love God, then ask to see the proof of the pudding — obedience to the Word of God. To put this in practical terms, if someone wants to be a leader in the church, then ask to see his submissive wife and obedient kids. He who does not love his children by requiring obedience from them is a liar.

HOW TO GET THERE FROM HERE

CHAPTER 4

THE GIVENS

N ow that we understand that God has priorities and that one of the highest ones is raising godly children, how do we get there from here? What principles do we find in the Word of God that will ensure that we are successful in training godly children for Him? First, make sure your own relationship with the Lord is deep and abiding. Do you have a consistent time with God? Are you confessing your sin as you commit it, rather than let it lay around to attract more? Are you studying the Word of God to understand what His commandments are, in order to obey them? Remember Deuteronomy chapter six. We are to love the Lord with all our heart, soul and strength and **then** we are to teach it to our children. How can you pass on a relationship with the Lord that you yourself do not have?

Second, is your marriage based on sound biblical principles? The Word of God is the standard by which all marriages must be measured. What we **think** a biblical marriage looks like is irrelevant. It does not matter what we have read, heard or seen purported to be a godly marriage. The only true criteria for a godly marriage is found in the Word of God. You may have had great Christian parents, but their marriage is only biblical to the point that it lines up with the Word of God.

A quick stroll through any Christian bookstore will reveal that marriage is a "hot" topic among Christians. Countless books are devoted to this subject and yet, most are not based on sound biblical principles. Sadly, most "Christian" marriage books fall into the category of the "Bible and something else" with very little emphasis on the Bible. The Bible and modern psychology. The Bible and learning to see life through your partner's eyes (as if we could or were ever commanded to do that!). The Bible and lots of heart-warming stories that praise egalitarianism and down-play the biblical roles of husband and wife.

The modern evangelical Christian is just as confused about biblical marriage as he is about the priorities of God. It stands to reason that without a biblical marriage, it is unlikely we will raise godly kids. There are exceptions, of course, but I would prefer to be obedient to God's Word concerning my marriage. I would rather not have my "sins visited on the third and fourth generations" (Exodus 34:7 and Numbers 14:18). So, before a father can fulfill one of God's highest priorities by raising godly children, he must first learn the biblical principles of marriage. This is not as hard as one might think. Open God's Word and let the Holy Spirit teach you. Look up "marriage" in a topical Bible and write down every passage where principles of marriage are taught. Make a few notes about each passage. Next, use cross references of these same passages to gain even more insight. Then, synthesize all of the information you have just learned and draw some principles.

God promises to give wisdom to those who ask, but you must be willing to obey whatever He shows you (James 1:5-8). **God's Word is not a salad bar.** You may not pick and choose which commandments and principles to obey based on which ones you feel most comfortable with. James sternly warns that we will not receive anything from the Lord with that type of attitude. And please do not use the excuse of "a different culture" to ignore difficult or inconvenient commandments. God's Word is powerful enough to transcend Old and New Testament culture. You will only be cheating yourself and causing your family untold grief by ignoring parts of God's Word, just because it was written in a different age!

Now, I am defining a deep relationship with the Lord and a biblical marriage as "givens" because they are essential to the task of raising godly children. Unfortunately, they are anything but "givens" in our culture today, even among believers. What do we do if we do not have a good marriage? What if our spouse is an unbeliever? What if we are new believers and do not know what the Word of God says about these "givens"? I have a simple answer for all of these questions. Repentance. We must acknowledge that we are sinners and ask forgiveness for our wrong attitudes and our wrong thinking. Make no mistake, unbiblical thinking is still a sin, even if we are ignorant of our error. Sin is **anything** that falls short of the glory of God. So, first repent and then, get busy implanting "the Word of God which is able to save your soul (realize there is more than justification implied in this verse)." We must realize that ignorance of God's principles does not absolve us from obedience. If we disobey, even in ignorance, there will be consequences. But we have a merciful God and if we are willing to confess our ignorance, our sin and our selfishness, He will begin the slow, painful process of conforming us to His Son according to (and through the agency of) His Word.

MOLDING OUR CHILDREN'S THINKING

Back to our original question. How do we fulfill God's highest calling to us as fathers — the raising of godly children? Aside from the "givens" of a good marriage and a good relationship with God, we must begin by **molding our children's world view**. Many sincere, but confused Christians recoil at the thought of actively shaping their children's thinking. "What right do I have to press my beliefs and values on another person made in the image of God?" I even had one father tell me that his job as a Christian parent was to "get out of the way" and minimize his influence on his children so that he would not "mess them up!"

Although this sounds spiritual, it is totally unbiblical. Your children are sinners like their father, Adam. They are not innocent and left to their own devices, will not follow after God (Isaiah 53:6). Contrary to popular belief (and most current movies), children are not the repositories of all innocence and wisdom. Proverbs 29:15 states that a child left to himself will bring shame to his mother. Proverbs 22:15 tells us that foolishness is bound up in your child's heart and it is your responsibility to remove it far from him. That will take a lot of work since even your regenerate children (those who place their faith in Jesus Christ and His work on the cross for the forgiveness of their sins) have a natural inclination toward sin. You will have to overcome not only the culture around them, but their sin nature as well.

How do we cause our children to begin thinking and evaluating as a Christian? We are to facilitate the transformation by the renewing of their minds in accordance with the Word of God (Romans 12:1-2). Are you teaching your children the Word of God? Deuteronomy 32:46-47 commands us to teach our children to obey all the words of His law. How can they obey what they do not know? One of the best things fathers can do for their families is to read to them daily from the Scriptures. It is one thing for your children to see youth group leaders or Sunday school teachers teach from the Word, but the greatest impact will occur when your children see you taking the lead in this most important of all activities.

Let's face it, your children realize something is truly important when Dad is involved in it. But training your children in God's Word should not be limited to formal devotional times. Deuteronomy 6:4-7 instructs us to train our children in the Word during normal activities as well. Are you engaging them in spiritual conversations while driving to soccer practice? Is it normative behavior for your family to discuss biblical issues around the dinner table? Do your children know how you think about certain issues?

PATTERNING OUR TEACHING AFTER THE GREAT TEACHER

Are you patterning the teaching of your children after the way God taught his children, the Israelites? Matt Whitling has an excellent application in his audio tape entitled Covenantal Discipline. Whitling states that when God gave a command to the Israelites, He usually followed the same general pattern. First, He would give them a command and then, He would give the attending blessings and curses for obedience and disobedience, respectively. However, He did not stop there. In order to help them obey, He would then give a hypothetical situation involving the command **before** they encountered the situation. For example, in Exodus 20:4-6, God commanded His people not to make idols nor to worship them. He then proceeded to tell them all of the blessings that would come to them if they obeyed and all the curses if they did not obey (see also Leviticus 26:4-39). Finally, He wrapped it up with a hypothetical situation in Exodus 34:12-17. He told them not to make a covenant with the inhabitants of the land **where they would be going in the very near future.**

Take heed to yourself, lest you make a covenant with the inhabitants of the land **where you are going**, lest it be a snare in your midst. But you shall destroy their altars, break their sacred pillars, and cut down their wooden images for you shall worship no other god, for the LORD, whose name is Jealous, is a jealous God, lest you make a covenant with the inhabitants of the land, and they play the harlot with their gods and make sacrifice to their gods, and one of them invites you and you eat of his sacrifice, and you take of his daughters for your sons, and his daughters play the harlot with their gods and make your sons play the harlot with their gods. You shall make no molded gods for yourselves. *(Exodus 34:12-17)*

God was giving His people training on how to avoid sin **before** they were in the heat of temptation. He did not just leave it in the theoretical realm, He made it very practical by describing a very real situation they would soon be facing. Are you giving your children hypothetical situations and asking them how they would react biblically **before** those situations arise? If your child were over at a friend's house and their mother asked him if he would like to watch a questionable movie, does your child know how to respond? We must teach our children to graciously respond to these types of situations at home **before** they are thrown into the pressure cooker of having to make hard decisions in front of peers and their parents. Have you talked to your children about purity? Waiting until your little girl is on her way out the door with a handsome boy is too late! We must be proactive instead of reactive when training our children in godliness.

Another way to mold your children's thinking is by watching videos on Christian apologetics together as a family and then, discussing them afterward. I took my family to a seminar on creation science by Ken Ham and was amazed at how much I had been duped by the culture around me. For example, if the world is indeed millions of years old, and dinosaurs roamed the earth long before man arrived, then what were those dinosaurs doing all that time? They were eating and being eaten. Some would inevitably succumb to disease and die. But wait a minute! When did death, disease and killing enter the world? The Bible says in Romans 5:12, that sin entered the world when Adam disobeyed and death came through sin. **Nothing died or became sick before Adam sinned!** If there were dinosaurs millions of years before Adam, then they would have had to be perfect, disease-free dinosaurs who never tasted death! God's Word is the ultimate authority by which **everything** must be measured! Have you taught your children that? Let God be true, but every man a liar (Romans 3:4).

One of the things that amazes me most when discipling young men in college, is how little they know about marriage and child rearing. Here are men who will be marrying and raising families in two or three years and have done nothing to prepare themselves for a task that is close at hand. They study intensely for their future careers, but somehow fail to study for the higher priority of raising a godly family. Are you preparing your children to be godly spouses and parents? Have you opened the Scriptures with them and made a list of the characteristics to look for in a prospective mate? How about their world view? Do they see raising godly kids as their highest priority? It is amazing how we give lip service to the importance of raising godly children and yet, we will choose careers that are hostile to this goal. Steer your children away from career paths that will remove them from their families for long periods of time. How can they disciple their future family if they are never around them?

If you encourage your daughters to attend college, counsel them to choose a field of study that will compliment their role in raising up intelligent, godly children. Discourage your daughters from choosing college majors that will inevitably result in jobs that rob from their families and set up a co-wage earnings struggle with their future husbands. Am I advocating that our daughters be naïve and uneducated? Certainly not! For, they will be the teachers of our future generations. They need to be thoroughly educated in the ways of God and be able to defend their little ones against the competing world views, which is no easy task! But please realize that modern education, especially at the collegiate level, rarely teaches one to think. In most cases, it is little more than advanced vocational training. Define your goal. If you want your daughters to be able to train up godly sons and daughters, then determine what they will need to accomplish this and choose a college or design a curriculum yourself to enable them to do so. If you feel inadequate to do this, pray with the intent to obey (James 1:5) and God will lead you to the right resources.

TEACHING OUR CHILDREN ABOUT FINANCES

Are you molding your children's thinking in the area of finances? Statistics show that finances are one of the main causes of marital strife. Teach your children early about the pitfalls of debt. Do a concordance study on the words "debt" or "surety" found in the Bible with your children and see what God has to say about the matter. You will be teaching them about finances as well as teaching them how to use the Bible to gain spiritual understanding on any given subject. Did you know that before World War I, almost ninety percent of the American people paid for their homes in cash. Even by World War II, the percentage was almost eighty percent. What has happened in the last sixty years? We have grown accustomed to buying more house than our income will allow. What it took our parents fifty years to accumulate, we want **now**. A new house has to have new furniture, right? Put it on the card! Teach your children to live off **one** income before they have children. This will make for a much smoother transition when Mom stays home as

God grants children to their young family. Along the same reasoning, train your sons to not view their wives as extra sources of income.

You may be thinking that it is too late. Perhaps you are in financial circumstances beyond your control. Some of you may be enslaved to debt and have no choice but to remain in your present situation, even though you know it is not the optimum setting for training godly kids. But God is a God who delivers the enslaved and sets the captive free, if we will only repent and cry out to Him. We may not see the deliverance in our lifetime, but we can train our children to be free men and women in theirs. Even if we must endure the consequences of foolish decisions, our children can stand on our shoulders and benefit from our sacrifices. Focus on the goal. The goal is to raise godly children who can think biblically and make decisions accordingly. It is worth the sacrifice. This is one reason I believe inheritances can be such a blessing if given and received with a godly spirit.

> A **good** man leaves an inheritance to his children's children, but the wealth of the sinner is stored up for the righteous. *(Proverbs 13:22)*

How wonderful it would be for our children not to start their families saddled with a long term mortgage! Are we to "spend our children's inheritance" as the bumper sticker proclaims, or can we bless them in a way that they can start their young families debt-free? Perhaps the idea of a dowry is not such an old-fashioned idea after all. If we have trained our children well, perhaps we can provide them with a "dowry" without encouraging laziness on their part or riding rough-shod over the authority and leadership of the young husband. I leave the details to you. Keep one thing in mind, however. It does not always take a sack of money to build a house. Sometimes it takes a lot of hard work, sweat and time.

TRAINING FUTURE LEADERS

Are you training your son to be the head of his future home? I am involved in a early morning discipleship group that takes me away from our family devotions one morning a week. Rather than have them skip the devotion in my absence, I am training my nine-year-old son to lead the family for that morning, while I am gone. Not only does this allow him to practice headship in a controlled environment, it also gives his older sisters the opportunity to show respect to their younger brother (the same respect they will be showing to their future husband someday). While we are on the subject of sons, realize that self-control taught and maintained at an early age translates into self-control when he is older and can do much more damage.

Do not be deceived, God is not mocked; **for whatever a man sows, that he will also reap**. For he who sows to his

flesh will of the flesh reap corruption, but he who sows to the Spirit will of the Spirit reap everlasting life. *(Galatians 6:7-8)*

The little boy who throws a temper tantrum and is not properly disciplined, will resort to more violent behavior when he is older. A young boy who is taught self-control in the areas of toys, cookies and little league baseball, is more likely to have that **same** self-control years later, when he is tempted by members of the opposite sex. Again, if you are diligent to train him to exercise self-control when he is young and the situations are fairly minor, he will then exercise the **same** self-control when he is older and can really get himself (and others) into trouble.

Another area to begin molding your children's thinking is current events. Read the paper with them and ask how certain situations line up with the Word of God. Watch commercials with them (with a ready hand on the remote) and ask them which world view is being taught. A great book to read on civil government is The Law, by Fredrick Bastiat. Although I do not know if Bastiat was a Christian, he has some timeless ideas on the practical application of God's commandments. One of his themes is "legalized plunder." If I, as an individual, am not allowed to take something by force that belongs to you (personal property), then how can a group of individuals do this to others and be morally right? Think of all the personal property (ie: money) that is taken from you by our federal government through the use of force and given to someone else, under the guise of altruism.

- Social Security
- Welfare
- Medicaid
- Medicare
- Public Education
- Public Broadcasting
- Seizure of private property for the "common good"

This does not even include intellectual property rights (think Microsoft), constitutional rights (you need a license to carry a gun) and the rights of private pursuit (you need a license to replace someone's commode!).

So, how do I train my kids in this area? I tell them to render to Caesar what is Caesar's, but render to God what is God's (Matthew 22:21). I will pay my social security tax (even though I am opposed to it), but I will **not** give my children over to the government to be educated in their pagan schools. If they passed a law prohibiting homeschooling, I would flee with my family to a different country. If they would not allow me to flee and tried to take my children by force in order to "educate" them, I would defend my family with my life. My children were not given to me by man. They were entrusted to me by a **much higher authority**, the Lord God Almighty! You may not go as far as I would, but have you thought through these issues? Think through them now, for you may soon be in a position where you will have to act. The time to do a Bible study on the biblical merits of personal defense is not when your wife is being attacked! Do your children know what you believe about these things? They will not learn what you think by osmosis. You must be able to articulate what you believe and why you believe it.

Early in our church history, a priest named Arius taught a heresy claiming that Jesus Christ was created by the Father. Another priest named Athanasias correctly surmised that if Jesus Christ is a created being, then He is not fully God, and we are still dead in our sins. Athanasias stood publicly against Arius, even when the whole church had accepted this heresy. One of his fellow priests asked him, "Athanasias, do you not know that the whole world is against you?" To which he replied, "Then let it be known that Athanasias is against the whole world!"

Who knows in what situation God may place your child when he is grown? He may be the next Athanasias. Are you training your children to think biblically and to stand firm against this evil culture? Are you training them to stand upon God's Word even when other Christians are duped by false teaching? Think beyond yourself. Think multi-generationally. Are you training your sons and daughters to not just to survive in enemy territory, but to overcome and take captives for their Lord Jesus Christ?!

A FATHER'S STEW

SOMETHING HAS TO CHANGE

CHAPTER 5

RADICAL LIFESTYLES

All of this molding and training requires tremendous amounts of work and time. But what if you do not have the time and when you do, you do not have the energy? We know from Scripture that God requires us to train our children to think and act in a manner worthy of Christ, but although the will is present, the flesh is weak. In reality, our lives are just too busy to adequately train a battle-ready soldier for Christ. There is a solution. If your current lifestyle does not allow adequate time to train your children in godliness, **then you need a new lifestyle!**

Paul states that although all things are lawful (provided they do not violate the commandments of Scripture), not all things are profitable (1 Corinthians 6:12). He goes on to say that he will not be mastered by anything. Activities that do not violate the Word of God are lawful, but they are not all profitable. And activities that impede the training of your children in godliness are outright sinful. Busyness is the mortal enemy of family discipleship. Take a long hard look at the activities your children are involved in. Your kids do not have to play every sport that your community offers! Let them choose one or two favorite things and reserve the rest of their time for family activities. Remember, you are training them **now** to be able to choose wisely in the **future** — to be able to discern the better from the best. What better way to practice this wisdom than by having to choose between two or more things they want to do? It is not their inalienable right to be entertained. It is their solemn duty to be godly. While I am on the subject, I encourage you to not allow the activity of one of your children to dominate the entire family's time. I have seen many families (especially in competitive sports) where one of the children's activity took so much time or took the family out of town on such a regular basis, that the other siblings became bitter and resentful. God put you in authority. Use it and use it wisely!

Although raising godly children is our number one priority, they should never feel that the home is centered around them. Children should feel grateful (and should be trained to express this gratefulness) to be allowed in your godly home and should understand that their activities will not be allowed to dominate this godly home. Make it a priority to eat dinner together and only deviate from this norm for the direst of circumstances. Your children need to see godly structure in your home, not random chaos where the most pressing need of the moment wins out. They will see plenty of that in the world and in other Christian's homes.

What better place to discuss biblical issues than at the dinner table? Make it normative behavior to discuss current events in light of Scripture. Spend time reading good books aloud to your kids, ones that extol virtue and godliness. Spend time just having fun with your kids. Play board games. Go camping. Have a least one family outing without their friends. I am not against having the neighborhood kids over, but there are times when a family needs to be together without distractions. Break the habit of watching the television after dinner.

GOD'S SOVEREIGNTY OVER OUR FREE TIME

Fathers, take a long hard look at your hobbies. Realize that there will be time enough to pursue our own interests after our children have grown and left to have families of their own. Again, we are speaking of priorities here. Our modern culture shouts at the top of its lungs, "You work hard. You deserve your down-time." Whole sectors of our economy run on that noble American principle: the right of recreation! Seriously, I am not against having fun, but we should be having fun with a purpose. There are some that might shame us into dropping all of our interests and concentrate solely on what delights our children. But remember, although they are the priority, they are not to be the center of attention. All activities should not revolve around them. You do not have to quit all of things you like to do. You can have fun and pass your passions to your children by involving them in the things you already enjoy doing.

If you are developing deep relationships with your children, they will naturally gravitate to things you like to do, because they long to be near you. Is that not how it is with the Father? As we grow in our relationship with Him, we begin to desire the things He holds most dear.

> Yes, in the way of Your judgments, O LORD, we have waited for You; the **desire of our soul is for Your name and for the remembrance of You**. *(Isaiah 26:8)*

A good example of this occurred with my oldest daughter, Ashley. I was a competitive pistol shooter for a few years. I would go to competitions once a month, but to stay at the top of my game, I would have to practice twice a week. All this practice began to pay off and one day, I won a competition and a check for fifty dollars. Bursting with pride, I told my wife about the fifty dollars and then she asked me how much the entry fee was. Eighty dollars, I replied meekly. I knew then I was not going to make a living shooting competitively!

However, when my daughter expressed an interest in shotgun shooting, I knew something would have to give. Although the pistol shooting was not taking an inordinate amount of time away from my family, I did not have the time to do both. Here was a chance to choose between what was good and what was best! I could still shoot, but I would have to lay down the pistol and pick up the shotgun in order to be involved with my daughter. I could have grumbled to God about having to give up my competitive pistol shooting, but I realized there are priorities that transcend my interests. Yet, with a little creativity, I can still pursue the things I am interested in, if I am willing to bend a little. Actually, this decision has returned blessing upon blessing, for now I have a new duck hunting partner!

My daughter was interested in shooting sports because I had shared my interests with her since she was a little girl. My second daughter does not have the same interest in shooting sports, but she has an interest in archery. Hey, archery is fine with me. At least there are targets and flying projectiles! The principle is not to abandon everything you like to do. Include your kids in your world. Share your interests and passions with them. However, if God puts His finger on an area in your life that is taking too much time away from your family, you must remember that your free time is not your own. It belongs to God. "For you were bought at a price; therefore glorify God in your body and in your spirit, which are God's" (1 Corinthians 6:20).

EDUCATING OUR CHILDREN

If our goal is to mold our children's thinking, and we know that it will require lots of work and lots of time, then homeschooling may be the answer. One of the laments of Christian parents who have children in the public school is the massive amount of time spent un-learning what their children have learned there. And this is only the stuff that you catch! There are many subtle and not so subtle messages that your children are absorbing in the public school that you will never see and most of this before your children are properly trained to discern between that which is biblical and that which is not. Do not underestimate the power of this culture to seduce your little ones (or yourselves!). Are there not ideas that you have held as little as two years ago that you now say, "How could I have thought that way?" How much more your children with less maturity in the Lord? Training our children in the Lord is hard enough without putting ourselves in the position of making up lost ground.

Suppose you were to stop a friend on his bicycle and ask where he is going. If he replied that he is riding to the neighborhood park just up the street, you think nothing of it. But, if he replied that he is headed to Alaska and you both live in Texas, you would begin to doubt his sanity! He is not using the right vehicle for the task at hand. Similarly, if your goal is children who can pass a standardized test and be able to do what they are told without thinking, then public school is probably the right vehicle for them. If your goal is loftier, then you need to look for something with a little more horse-power. Again, if you want children who will not merely survive in this culture, but will overcome and take captives for Jesus Christ, then they will need a distinctly Christian education. One of the most dangerous aspects of public schools is not the drugs, guns and ungodly sex education. It is not even the lie that homosexuality is an acceptable alternative. It is the lie that our children can be properly educated without reference to God. Douglas Wilson expounds upon this concept in his book, <u>Excused Absence: Should Christian Kids Leave Public Schools?</u>

When our children attend government schools, they are told to learn math, but not to learn the central thing about math — that God is a God of order and that in Him all things consist. They are told to learn history, but not the most important thing about history — that Jesus Christ lived a perfect life, died an efficacious death, rose powerfully, and ascended majestically to the right hand of the Father.

When God is excluded from the classroom, we are not merely remaining silent about God. We are teaching children that they may safely disregard Him. Whether or not God exists, the lesson goes, His existence is irrelevant to what we are doing here. So when God is omitted, we are not silent about Him; rather we are teaching the children in the most convincing way possible that God is irrelevant. They can safely omit Him when it is convenient to do so.

If we truly want a vehicle with the horse-power to fully educate our children to think for themselves and honor the Lord, then homeschooling may be the answer. Homeschooling fits perfectly with the idea of altering our lifestyles to maximize the training of our little ones to godliness. It provides the unique one-on-one training ground that can not be matched by public schools, private schools or even Christian schools. If you want to know exactly what is being taught to your child and how it is being presented, what better way than by doing it yourself? However, be forewarned! Our culture, which preaches tolerance to all, is very **intolerant** of the idea of your educating your own children. After all, education is the modern savior and the State will have no other gods before it.

Or do you not realize that man is intrinsically good and the reason we have poverty, violence and disease is because of a lack of education? If only every one were properly educated, mankind could stamp out every evil in this world and we could all live in peace and harmony. But in order for this to occur we must all be educated **in the same way**. We can not have some children educated in one way and others in another. And most certainly we can not have them think for themselves, for that might upset the whole apple cart. No, we will educate all in the same subjects and in the same manner, away from the meddlesome influence of parents, in order to create the perfect citizen. One who will do what he is told and will not question the culture, especially in the light of that intolerant book, the Bible!

Now I am not saying that every teacher, principal or even school administrator has evil intentions for your child. The sad fact is, having been raised in the public schools themselves, they are probably not even conscious of the agenda that is being propagated. But it is there none-the-less. Just remember, Jesus said that he who is not for Him is against Him and the public schools have shut Him out with a vengeance. There is nothing neutral about public education. God has revealed their agenda in recent times and they do not even bother to hide it anymore.

"But, even if we see the danger of having the unbelievers educate our children, how can we go so far as to home school? Isn't that for Christians who isolate themselves and have their own backyard bomb shelters?" Let's look at a few of the objections the world (and, unfortunately, the church) will use to dissuade you from homeschooling.

HOW CAN YOU TEACH YOUR CHILDREN WHEN YOU DON'T HAVE A DEGREE IN EDUCATION?

First, we should look at the promise found in Scripture. If God has given you children and He commands you to thoroughly educate the children *whom He has given you,* will He not provide all the resources necessary to thoroughly educate those children to His glory? This does not mean you have to be an expert in every subject. It does mean, however, that you must take responsibility for your child's education, for you will one day give an accounting to the Lord. With all of the excellent books, resources on the internet and local home school cooperatives and organizations, you will be able to oversee your child's education even if you do not teach every subject. Of course, there should be no occasion for laziness. Remember that we are training our sons and daughters to one day train their own sons and daughters. We must train them to fight in hand-to-hand combat with the ideas of the world. Even if you do not have a college degree, remember that the loving shepherd tends the sheep better than the hireling with a master's degree.

WHAT ABOUT SOCIALIZATION? DON'T YOU WANT YOUR CHILDREN TO BE ABLE TO INTERACT WITH OTHERS?

The premise here is that homeschoolers never leave the home. On the contrary, because of the less rigid schedule (teaching for standardized tests, finding chaperones, hiring bus drivers, getting permission slips, worrying about students running away, etc.), homeschoolers are able to take many more educational field trips and interact with a greater diversity of people. Think of all the time that is wasted at a public school: the time spent riding on the school bus, changing class rooms every hour, extended bathroom breaks, constant interruptions, etc. By having more concentrated time for their studies, as well as a lower teacher/pupil ratio, homeschoolers are able to do their work more quickly and thus, have more time for extracurricular activities such as art, music, hobbies, sports and drama.

A FATHER'S STEW

In our quest for socialization, we must not forget that not all socialization is biblical. The Scripture teaches that "bad company corrupts good morals" (1 Corinthians 15:33). Also, "a companion of fools will be destroyed" (Proverbs 13:20). And what do you call a room of twenty fifth-grade boys? Having taught them, I can attest that it is a room full of fools! Again the Bible teaches that "foolishness is bound up in the heart of a child and the rod of correction will drive it far from him (Proverbs 22:15)." What good thing can a fifth-grade boy learn from nineteen other fifth-grade boys? Now I am not saying that children should not be allowed to play with others his own age, but we do not have to actively segregate them into isolated peer-groups. We joke about the monosyllabic teenager who can only grunt in reply to queries from adults and yet, it is actually an indictment of grouping them according to age. For all the vaunted cries of "socialization," public school children are usually much less adept than their homeschool counter parts at relating to others of various ages. (Another indication that the our culture discriminates against homeschoolers is that I can not even type the word "homeschool" without the spell check on my computer flagging it as an incorrect word. I guess Bill Gates was not homeschooled!)

SHOULDN'T YOUR CHILDREN BE SALT AND LIGHT IN THE PUBLIC SCHOOL SYSTEM?

I usually hear this one from the dads. "I want my kid to be a witness. How is he ever going to learn to defend his faith if he doesn't go to a public school?" I usually respond by asking him what training program he is using with his kids. To which I inevitably receive a blank stare. It would be unthinkable to send an **adult** soldier into combat without massive amounts of training and yet we are more than willing to send our children into combat with little or no training at all. How shameful! If you are so concerned about the evangelism of the public school system, are you leading your children in family devotions before they go to school? Are you training them in Christian apologetics? Have you taught them the basics of the gospel backwards and forwards? Have you required them to read the entire Bible, cover to cover, numerous times? If you have done these things and they exhibit an extraordinary amount of Christian maturity, **then** you can send them into battle. Until then, do not justify your apathy towards training your children in godliness by claiming the moral high ground of evangelism.

Please, do not misunderstand me. I am not adverse to my children being around unbelievers. Paul states that we are to associate with unbelievers (1 Corinthians 5:9-11). However, I want my children to associate with unbelievers under my guidance. Through baseball, soccer, basketball and shooting sports, we have become friends with many unbelievers, but I have always played an active role in each of these activities. My children have learned to interact with unbelievers in a controlled environment, under my authority. We then discuss this in a biblical light, for one day soon, they will no longer be under my authority and they will have to fight on their own. However, they will have been trained and tested in situations that were not overwhelming, because I was with them. Actually, this is one of the dangers of the modern youth group. Because we assume that it is "Christian," we let our guard down and allow our children to be seduced away. Fathers, you are responsible for the training of your children. Do not allow anyone, not even the church, to cause your children to fall away from the truths found in the Word of God.

> But even if we, **or an angel from heaven**, preach any other gospel to you than what we have preached to you, let him be accursed. *(Galatians 1:8)*

WHAT WILL HAPPEN TO THE PUBLIC SCHOOL SYSTEM IF ALL OF THE CHRISTIANS PULL OUT?

Who cares! What does it matter if an institution that has rejected God in totality crumbles under its own weight? Why should Christians have a vested interest in a system that seeks at every turn to strip our little ones of the godly heritage we are trying to give them? What do we owe the public school system? They take our money at the point of a bayonet and use that money to seduce our children away from us and God. You can not accept "free" education without the strings.

Do not be unequally yoked together with unbelievers. For what fellowship has righteousness with lawlessness? And what communion has light with darkness? And what accord has Christ with Belial? Or what part has a believer with an unbeliever? And what agreement has the temple of God with idols? For you are the temple of the living God. As God has said: "I will dwell in them and walk among them. I will be their God, and they shall be My people." Therefore "**Come out from among them and be separate**, says the Lord. Do not touch what is unclean, and I will receive you." *(2 Corinthians 6:14-17)*

It is one thing to associate with unbelievers for the purpose of evangelism. It is quite another to let them educate your kids. Even if your children have Christian teachers in the public school system, realize that if they taught in the way the Bible instructs Christians to teach, they would lose their jobs. They must hide their light under a bushel! These Christian teachers would do well to heed the warning in Titus:

For the grace of God that brings salvation has appeared to all men, **teaching us** that, denying ungodliness and worldly lusts, we should live soberly, righteously,

and godly in the present age, looking for the blessed hope and glorious appearing of our great God and Savior Jesus Christ, who gave Himself for us, that He might redeem us from every lawless deed and purify for Himself His own special people, zealous for good works. **Speak these things, exhort, and rebuke with all authority. Let no one despise you.** *(Titus 2:11-15)*

A WARNING

Although homeschooling provides an unparalleled opportunity to disciple your children, a word of caution is in order. If you are pulling your child out of a public school because of his worsening behavior, do not expect the problem to disappear when you begin homeschooling. Your children act the way they do because you have trained them that way. You may not have set out to have a surly son, but when you allow that behavior to continue or make excuses for it, then you are actually teaching him that surliness is profitable. Although public school influences may have contributed to your child's worsening behavior, please realize that **bad behavior starts in the home**. Unless you are willing to repent before God and begin to discipline in accordance with Scripture, you are in for a very rough road and you will probably not see the blessings of homeschooling.

If you do not see the lack of discipline in your child as a major problem or feel that it is "just a phase that he is going through," then you would do well to heed the example of Eli in the second chapter of 1 Samuel. Eli scolded his sons for their disobedience, but it was too little, too late. When all was said and done, Eli, his two sons and 38,000 Israelites lost their lives because of his failure to discipline his sons. The most telling verse is in 1 Samuel 2:29. God told Eli that by not disciplining his sons, "You have honored your sons more than Me." Do you honor your children more than you honor God? Do you know better than God what your child requires? As parents, our sins have far reaching consequences in this life and the life to come. God promises to visit the sins of the father on the future generations. Keep those sin accounts short!

PATRIARCHAL EXAMPLES?!?

CHAPTER 6

DO AS I SAY, NOT AS I DO

For a father, one of the most sobering realizations in the Word of God is how many of the patriarchs had rebellious children. If Samuel, David and Solomon had rebellious kids, what hope do we have? I believe God revealed these men, with their warts and all, for our instruction. Notice from the last chapter that Eli's sons were adults. His responsibility and accountability did not stop when his sons reached the age of eighteen or left the house. We have a nasty habit of excusing bad parenting when it is manifested **outside** of the home. Eli's sons did not suddenly become bad once they left his home. We can rightly surmise that Eli had made a practice of **not** rebuking, disciplining or training his sons during their upbringing and the Bible faithfully records the fruit of that type of parenting. Solomon told us to "chasten our children while there is still hope and not set our heart on their destruction" (Proverbs 19:18). In today's vernacular, that means spank your children while they are still young enough for it to do some good, and you will not set them up for a big fall when they are older. Actually, I like it better the way Solomon said it!

One would think that the prophet Samuel would have learned the lesson of training up godly sons, for he was the one who prophesied to Eli that his sons would die due to their disobedience. However, the Bible records that Samuel's sons rebelled as well (1 Samuel 8:3-4). In fact, the disobedience of his sons was the main reason the Israelites asked for a king. The Lord was greatly displeased with this request, for He knew that the people were rejecting His authority and clamoring to be under the authority of a man (1 Samuel 8:7). Countless men and women will spend eternity separated from God as a result of the idol worship instigated by many of these evil Israeli kings. I hope you are beginning to see the huge consequences for not raising godly children. These will affect not only our own families, but others as well. In addition, the kingdom of God will be affected by the way we raise our families — for better or worse. Some may still argue that all we can do is our best. We can try to raise our children in a godly way, but there are no guarantees. I again refer back to Proverbs 22:6.

> Train up a child in the way he should go,
> and when he is old he will not depart from
> it. *(Proverbs 22:6)*

Whether you take the above verse as a promise or a proverb, **it should still be the norm for Christian parents.**

Just as Paul exhorted the Ephesians to walk in a manner worthy of their calling, we should expect our teenage children to honor and obey their parents. When they do not, we should not make excuses or glory in the fact they are "pushing the limits of their freedom," we should realize that something is wrong and search the Scriptures for the answer. We have already spent a lot of time on training your children, so I will not belabor the point. We should avoid at all costs, however, the complacency that we see in the Christian culture today of accepting bad behavior from our children and honoring them more than we honor God.

As if Eli and Samuel were not enough of an example of how not to raise your children, we are presented with David. Here was a "man after God's own heart" who raised three wicked sons and another who apostatized. When David's son, Amnon, raped his half sister, Tamar (David's daughter by another marriage), the Bible tells us that David became very angry (2 Samuel 13:21). Apparently, that is all that David did because there is no mention of a rebuke or jail term or anything. In fact, David's other son, Absalom (Tamar's brother), became so angry at the lack of punishment, that he killed Amnon two years later under the guise of inviting him to a party. After a brief stint of running from the law, he came back and was unable to gain an audience with his father, David. Absalom then set another's field on fire to get his father's attention, unlawfully assumed his father's throne, raped his father's concubines in public view, tried to kill his father and finally, wound up being destroyed himself.

One of the contributing factors to all of this mess was the fact that David had five wives — and this before he sinned with another man's wife, Bathsheba. The difficulty of raising godly children when working on our third marriage and throwing children from several different marriages into one house, should be obvious to all. Unfortunately, our churches which focus only on the felt need of the moment, are oblivious to this. If you find yourself in divorce situation, realize there is forgiveness in Christ. However, the consequences of the sin of divorce do not go away. You will have a long road ahead of you trying to raise godly children in such an environment. If you are not in that situation yet, but are considering getting a divorce, you would do well to heed the warning of Malachi.

> And this is the second thing you do:
> You cover the altar of the LORD with tears,
> With weeping and crying;
> So He does not regard the offering anymore,
> Nor receive it with goodwill from your hands.
> Yet you say, "For what reason?"
> Because the LORD has been witness
> Between you and the wife of your youth,
> With whom you have dealt treacherously;
> Yet she is your companion
> And your wife by covenant.
> But did He not make them one,
> Having a remnant of the Spirit?

And why one?
He seeks godly offspring.
Therefore take heed to your spirit,
And let none deal treacherously with the
wife of his youth.
"For the LORD God of Israel says
That He hates divorce,
For it covers one's garment with violence,"
Says the LORD of hosts.
"Therefore take heed to your spirit,
That you do not deal treacherously."
(Malachi 2:13-16)

Why does God no longer regard your offering? Because you have dealt treacherously with the wife of your youth. And why did He make you one? Because He desires godly offspring. According to this passage, one of the main reasons for marriage is to have godly children. **If we fail to have godly children, we are failing in our marriages.** The converse can also be true. If we fail in our marriages, we make raising godly children very difficult at best. That is why God hates divorce. It destroys marriage and greatly diminishes the chances of raising godly children, both of which bring Him glory.

Perhaps the most telling verse in regards to David's parenting skills is found in regards to his third wicked son, Adonijah.

Then Adonijah the son of Haggith exalted
himself, saying, "I will be king"; and he

prepared for himself chariots and horsemen, and fifty men to run before him. (**And his father had not rebuked him at any time by saying, "Why have you done so?"** He was also very good-looking. His mother had borne him after Absalom.) *1 Kings 1:5-7*

David never rebuked his sons. David feared confrontation more than he loved his sons. How are you in this area? Do you love your children enough to rebuke them? Do you love your children enough to spank them? The Bible teaches that a man who will not spank his children **hates** them (Proverbs 13:24). Or do you know more than God? Are your methods of discipline more effective than God's?

BIBLICAL METHODS OF INSTRUCTION

I am not saying that corporal punishment is the only option for every situation, but I will say that nothing is more effective when children are little. You may not use a circular saw in every situation when building a house, but you will use a circular saw on every house you build. And during the first stages of construction, you will use it the majority of the time.

One of the reasons I do not like time-out is that it unnecessarily prolongs the discipline. If your child willfully defies you (such as touching something you have told him not to), then give him a few sharp stings to the back of the hand with a wooden spoon. You can then hug him afterward to restore fellowship. When you send your child to time-out for an extended period of time, the break in fellowship is prolonged as well. Spanking is instantaneous. With time-out, he may have forgotten the offense before he even reaches the time-out corner.

Grounding also falls into this category. The goal of discipline is to modify behavior and then restore fellowship as quickly as possible. Why drag out the break in fellowship? Now if grounding fits the crime, such as suspending computer privileges for abuse of those privileges, I am fine with that. However, to ground a child for failure to obey a command is counter productive. Just spank them, get it over with and restore the fellowship. Be creative with your discipline. If your child forgets to feed the dog, let them go without supper so they can appreciate the importance of feeding a loved one. Make the punishment fit the crime.

Although I have been addressing discipline here, it goes without saying that it is much better (and effective in the long run) to consistently **train** your children to behave correctly rather than to discipline after they have failed. The key word is "train." Training is very different than disciplining. You can use a light switch on the back of a child's hand to teach him not to touch an object, just as you would use a pinch collar to train a dog to walk beside you. There is no anger involved in either of these. It is simply behavior modification. You can also use the same method for temper tantrums, sullen moods, nap time and stealing toys, to name a few. The idea is to train the child towards godly obedience by convincing him that the temporary pleasure of disobedience is not worth the price. Proper training does not wait until you are at the boiling point. It is methodical and consistent. It takes all of the anger out of the situation. No amount of discipline can make up for the lack of training.

One more caveat before we leave this topic. Hebrews 12:9 states that since "we have had human fathers who corrected us, and we paid them respect. Shall we not much more readily be in subjection to the Father of spirits and live?" What is the correlation between our earthly fathers and our heavenly Father? If our earthly fathers fail to correct us and we fail to pay them respect, how will we ever learn to submit to our unseen heavenly Father? Fathers have an awesome responsibility to faithfully administer godly discipline, for this is how our children learn to relate to our almighty God. As scary as it may seem, our little ones are learning about God by looking at us. A father who raises his children biblically is an immense blessing to them. On the other hand, no one can screw up a child's view of God like Dad can.

DRASTIC MEASURES

Deepening your relationship with God and training your children in godliness should be your highest priorities in life. They supercede all others priorities including work, ministry, church and hobbies. We have already discussed changing our lifestyles to conform with God's priorities,

but may I take it a step further? **If your present job does not allow you enough time to train your children in godliness, then you need a new job.** It may not pay as much, or be as prestigious, but look at the cost of the job that does not give you the flexibility to disciple your kids. You will be failing at God's highest priority for you as a parent and you will be disqualifying yourself for any leadership in the church body (1 Timothy 3:4-5). Am I being radical enough? Do you see the importance of raising godly kids? It transcends all other responsibilities, for this is how God has chosen to subdue the world for Himself! Now, the point here is not to rush out and find a new job. First, circumcise your lifestyle. If after you "lay aside every weight, and the sin which so easily ensnares us (Hebrews 12:1)", then you may find that your current job keeps you from spending the time required to train your children in righteousness. If that is the case, then pursue a job (or jobs) that allows you to adequately disciple your children. We will pursue this idea more thoroughly in the next chapter.

Remember, training soldiers takes time. The world tells you not to worry about the time spent away from your kids. You can make up the **quantity** of time you are separated from them by stressing the **quality** of time when you are together. Not only is this a lie, it defies common sense. Think about the time your four-year-old asked you to tell him about God. What about the day your teenager asked how you knew when your wife was the "one"? Or how about the time your eight-year-old asked you how to become a

Christian? When these "windows of opportunity" present themselves, you or your wife need to be there to put something through the window. Those windows will stay open only for a moment and then they close, leaving behind blessed memories or bitter regret. We can not control when the windows open or how long they will remain that way. We can not schedule those moments in our day-timers for a more convenient time. God is the One Who opens and shuts the windows and we must be ready for the opportunities. Are you ready for those "windows of opportunities"? Have you prepared yourself spiritually to be able to put something worthwhile in? Will you even be around when the opportunity arrives or will someone without your Christian world view seize the opportunity and sow tares among the wheat. Make no mistake, we are involved in a life and death struggle for the spiritual health of our children. You will either prevail through God's grace or be prevailed upon. There is no middle ground. No quarter will be given.

The Second Ingredient: Work

A FATHER'S STEW

THE PROBLEM WITH WORK

I chose this ingredient as second, not because it is second in importance, but because it so dominates our day to day lives. If not kept in proper perspective, work will overpower the other two ingredients; family and ministry.

MY STORY

I owned my own construction company for seventeen years. By all of the world's standards, I was living the free life. To an outsider it looked as if I was free to decide who I worked for, what projects I took, when I went to the office and how much money I made. But little more than a passing glance revealed a dark secret. To keep the money coming in, I had to have work and **lots of it!** Bringing in lots of work meant lots of hours meeting with prospective clients and estimating their projects. Actually, selling the work was only the beginning. Once sold, the work had to be performed on time and on budget. At first, I enjoyed the rush; the problem solving, thinking fast on my feet, the competitive nature of selling and the money. I immersed myself in building my company by studying remodeling magazines, attending seminars and going to remodeling conventions. I became very good at selling and producing remodeling — building my company into one of the largest remodeling companies in the area.

But the demands of the company began to take their toll. The client's demands always exceeded what I could deliver. I began working longer hours trying to keep up, taking precious time away from my family. I also began to have more flare-ups with my subcontractors, trying to push them to meet the clients' unrealistic time or quality expectations. I would come home sullen and moody, just begging for a fight with my wife. I began to bark at the kids more. Why wasn't my family more grateful for all that I was providing them? Couldn't they be a little more sympathetic to my bad moods, knowing it was a small price to pay for our family's success?

Deep down I knew this was not God's best, but what could I do? I had to put beans on the table, didn't I? "But you have your own business! You call your own shots! You are your own boss!" Yes, I had my own business and **other people** still determined:

- Who I worked for:
  Everyone! I needed a large volume of work to keep the money flowing. I could not afford to be picky.

- When I went to work:
  Early! I had projects to estimate!

A FATHER'S STEW

- When I went home:
  Late! I had calls and appointments to make!

- When I took time off:
  Actually, it took so long to get everything ready before I could leave, and there were so many problems when I came back, that vacations were exhausting. My wife and kids could tell you that I was no fun on vacations anyway (I was always worried about what was going wrong when I was away). I was quickly loosing the freedoms which had prompted me to start my own business in the first place!

Of course I began to get frequent headaches. My stomach was in constant knots. Why bother with the spoon when you can drink Pepto-Bismol straight from the bottle (the only bad thing was that little chalky ring around the top)? As soon as I woke up in the morning, the dread of going to work would descend like a fog. I would secretly rejoice when there were no calls on the answering machine. Even though that meant no new jobs, it also meant no complaining clients either. The one aspect of business I enjoyed the most was closing the deal. Even this began to lose its luster, because selling a job meant one more client to keep happy. Selling a remodeling job meant more hassles, more complaining and more stress. When I was not irritable, I was tired and listless. But I was self-employed! I worked for myself! And I was also completely unhappy. I knew I was in trouble when a man from Africa asked me what I did for a living. I glibly replied, "I destroy perfectly good kitchens and replace them with very expensive kitchens for women who will never cook again." He shook his head and exclaimed, "America is a very strange place!" And indeed it is. But dissatisfaction with work is not the exclusive property of this author, this country or even these times. It has been around for a long time.

SOLOMON'S STORY

It is comforting to know that I am not the only one who has ever had a problem with work. Solomon wrote of the problem of work in the Book of Ecclesiastes:

> Therefore **I hated life** because the work that was done under the sun was distressing to me, for all is vanity and grasping for the wind. Then I **hated all my labor** in which I had toiled under the sun, because I must leave it to the man who will come after me. And who knows whether he will be wise or a fool? Yet he will rule over all my labor in which I toiled and in which I have shown myself wise under the sun. This also is vanity. Therefore I turned my heart and **despaired of all the labor in which I had toiled** under the sun. For there is a man whose labor is with wisdom, knowledge, and skill; yet he must leave his heritage to a man who

has not labored for it. This also is vanity and a great evil. For what has man for all his labor, and for the striving of his heart with which he has toiled under the sun? **For all his days are sorrowful, and his work burdensome; even in the night his heart takes no rest**. This also is vanity. *(Ecclesiastes 2:17-20)*

Solomon hated life. Think about that. Here was the wealthiest man in the wealthiest country of the world at that time. Scripture says that gold and silver were as common as stones during his reign (2 Chronicles 1:15). He was also the wisest man to have ever lived. He had wealth, power and lots of women. And yet, Solomon had a problem. He hated his job. He also hated his life. One of the reasons Solomon hated his work is found in the passage above.

Then I hated all my labor in which I had toiled under the sun, because I must leave it to the man who will come after me. And who knows whether he will be wise or a fool? Yet he will rule over all my labor in which I toiled and in which I have shown myself wise under the sun.

Notice why Solomon is upset. He does not want to leave his work to another man. What especially irks him is the thought of someone else ruling over **his** labor in which **he** has toiled and in which **he** has shown **himself** wise. Who is missing in this equation? Had not God, through His sovereignty, placed Solomon in line to be the king of Israel? Had not God allowed him to be chosen over his older brothers to rule? And Who gave Solomon his superior intellect and wisdom? Solomon was trying to extract from work something that work was never meant to give. Never in Scripture will we find work as a legitimate avenue to our personal glory. Glory is the sole property of God.

Scripture makes it very clear that relationship with Him is the priority, and work is designed to be an outward manifestation of that relationship (Matthew 6:33). Solomon's priority in work was to bring glory to himself, not his Creator. He wanted everyone to see his labor and remark how well he had shown himself wise under the sun. Does this sound familiar? Our culture worships fame and fortune. We even have television shows that take us into their houses, when our gods are not home. Frustration is inevitable when we substitute work for a deep and abiding relationship with our Creator. We will fall into the same trap as Solomon; for work is to glorify God, not ourselves.

Yet, there was another reason Solomon "hated his labor." He was concerned about the one who would take over his work. Would that man be wise or foolish? He wanted his glory to continue beyond his lifetime and saw the continuation of his work as a vehicle for this. If no one could be found to ably manage the work, then all was for naught. Even though he suffered from "greed for glory," Solomon was actually following a legitimate biblical principle. He was thinking multi-generationally, though in his case, it was primarily for himself. Do we think multi-generationally? Is there someone to take over our "work" when we leave the scene? I am not talking about someone to take over your nine o'clock shift at the factory. I am talking about your life's work. What is your life's work? Your occupation is a part of that life's work and should be done for the glory of God, but I am talking about the legacy you will leave for the kingdom of God. Are you leaving godly, obedient children who will in turn leave more godly, obedient children? Where are the young believers you have poured your life into and led to Christian maturity? Have you imparted this same vision of discipleship to them in such a way that they will do the same with other believers?

Why was Solomon so afraid to leave his work to another? Where was the man he had carefully trained and groomed to take over his "works." If his glory was so important to him, why did he not have enough foresight to properly and laboriously train another to assume this important responsibility. **Where was his son?**

Although Solomon had written the book of Proverbs — the greatest instruction manual for young men ever written — his son apparently had not taken it to heart. We read in First Kings chapter twelve that Rehoboam (Solomon's son) rejected the advice of the wise elders who served under his father and instead took the advice of the young men he had grown up with. The result was the tearing in two of a kingdom that had enjoyed peace for more than forty years. The son had destroyed the father's work. This should be a lesson to all. We can not simply give our children a how-to manual and expect to get the job done. As I said in the last chapter, training godly children takes inordinate amounts of time. Growing Christian maturity in young fathers, husbands and college men wears you out physically, mentally and emotionally. Sure Solomon was busy, but aren't we all? However, observe the price he paid for not training his son in godliness. Solomon hated life. All was vanity to him. It will be the same for you if you do not take God's priorities seriously. But I digress, back to the problems of work.

WORK-RELATED DAMAGE

Although I could see the emotional and physical toll exacted upon me by my work, I was blind to the spiritual devastation that was occurring as well. My philosophy about work and life could best be summed up in a conversation I had with my Mom. She had called to say that she was leaving her current job because it did not fulfill her anymore. After her repeated tries to convince me why she needed to quit, I grew frustrated and asked her, "Why do you think they call it work, Mom? The purpose of a job is to put beans on the table and pay the rent. Anything else is gravy." You see, I believed that only a lucky few really enjoyed their work. God never promised fulfillment in work, or so I thought, so why should I expect to enjoy my job? My secret to happiness (or at least the lack of pain) was to isolate my job from my family and my ministry. If I could just compart-mentalize my life so that work did not touch anything else, I could then endure the stress. If I could just figure out a way to leave all of the stress and anxiety at the office, I could enjoy peace and tranquility at home.

But there was a problem with this. It did not work and it was not biblical. God never intended for us to separate our lives into little compartments over which we have sovereign control. He is the Lord of this earth and He is the Lord of our lives, whether we choose Him to be or not. Many evangelicals have a misguided notion that Jesus will be the Lord of our lives only when we give Him that authority. Either He is the omnipotent God or He is not. You may be disobeying Him in your work, but He is not handcuffed by your disobedience. He will have His way with your help or in spite of your rebellion, but He will have His way.

> The king's heart is in the hand of the LORD, like the rivers of water; He turns it wherever He wishes. *(Proverbs 21:1)*

I could not keep the problems at work from spilling over into the other areas of my life. My personal time with God, which was already inconsistent at best, was being pushed aside for more urgent business concerns. When I did have a quiet time, my mind would wander to the things I needed to do at the office that day. I tried switching my personal time with God to the evenings (because I was going to the office earlier by now), but I just did not have the energy to focus after being at the office all day. Because my mind and heart were focused elsewhere, I knew I was missing opportunities and leadings from the Holy Spirit. When I was not at the office, I was thinking about the office. I was too busy to lead a family devotion in the morning and too tired to lead one at night. I began to realize that the bulk of my spiritual input into my children was a short night time prayer and hauling them to church on Sundays to be taught by someone else! Clearly, this style of work was not God's best for me. And I dare say that it is probably not God's best for you! Unfortunately, work-related damage was not something I had a monopoly on. It is a wide spread phenomenon:

- 40% of workers report that their job is "very or extremely stressful."
  Survey by Northwestern National Life

- One-fourth of employees view their jobs as the number one stressor in their lives.
  Survey by Northwestern National Life

- Three-fourths of employees believe the worker has more on-the-job stress than a generation ago.
  Princeton Survey Research Associates

- Problems at work are more strongly associated with health complaints than are any other life stressor — more so than even financial or family problems.
  St. Paul Fire and Marine Insurance Company

- Industrial stress claims are the fastest growing type of Workers' Compensation claim today. While the incidence of disabling injuries dropped 8% since 1980, the frequency of stress claims increased almost 540% for the same period. Between 1979 and 1988 (the last year that statistics are available in California) job-related mental stress claims reported to employers increased by nearly 700%. It was estimated in 1988 that the overall cost to employers and insurance companies (and ultimately the general public) would be greater than $460 million for these claims.

  www.well-net.com

- 75% of all medical complaints are stressed related. Stress-related injuries account for more than 70% of all absenteeism and costs the economy nearly $100 billion annually.

  American Institute of Stress

- 40% of job turnover is due to stress.

  www.stress.org

- 60 to 80% of accidents on the job are stress related.

  www.stress.org

WORK IS NOT
CHAPTER 8 **THE PROBLEM**

LABORING FOR THE WIND

The statistics in the last chapter should not really surprise us. Solomon wrote of work-related damage over 3000 years ago.

> And this also is a severe evil— just exactly as he came, so shall he go. And what profit has **he who has labored for the wind**? All his days he also eats in darkness, and he has much **sorrow and sickness and anger**. *(Ecclesiastes 5:16-17)*

In the passage above, Solomon speaks of laboring for the wind and its attending consequences. What does it mean to labor for the wind? The idea is akin to our modern day expression of "nailing down Jello." When the Lord is not given preeminence, we can put all of our energies into a task and never quite accomplish it. We can pour all of our emotions into a work and never be satisfied. Tending the garden was never meant to take the place of Adam's deep dependence on God. The work was a result of the relationship and therefore, found its meaning in the relationship. Our "work" should be an outworking of our deep and abiding walk with our Creator. This is why two men can do essentially the same work and one labor in righteousness and the other labor for the wind.

But what are the consequences for having the wrong world view concerning work. Look at the preceding verse again. Solomon says we will eat in darkness. We are a nation who eats in darkness, ignoring the One who provided the bounty in the first place. Spiritual blindness has come upon us and we do not see the spiritual realities around us. We do not avail ourselves of spiritual opportunities because the manner in which we pursue work in particular and life in general, has clouded our vision. We are truly a people whom God has "given our request, but sent leanness into our souls (Psalms 106:15)." The modern evangelical church has failed to realize that God's judgment is not just around the corner — it is already here!

As an aside, we Americans operate under the misguided assumption that what we don't know can't hurt us. But God will hold us accountable for reading, understanding and applying His Word. Being unaware of what the Bible teaches, concerning the strict qualifications of elders, does not mean we will escape the consequences (spiritual and natural) of having carnal men lead our churches. Even if we do not understand why the Bible states that a woman should not teach or pastor over men (1 Timothy 2:12), it will be no consolation when we finally discover "why" a generation later, when our sons are unable to lead. If we ignore the admonition in Deuteronomy 6 to train our children in the ways of the Lord, He will not wave a magic wand and erase the consequences of our churches not taking this passage seriously. In short, we are responsible for all of Scripture whether we agree with it or not — whether we understand it or not. Not knowing or understanding biblical principles does not exclude us from the consequences of disobeying them. Eating in darkness is a very risky endeavor.

> All his days he also eats in darkness, and he has much **sorrow and sickness and anger**.

Notice that the man in the above passage is eating. Hard work, even when performed in an unbiblical manner or with an unbiblical attitude, may provide enough to eat, but it will be a bitter meal indeed! Today's lunch special is sorrow, sickness and anger. Look closely at your choices on the menu. Laboring after the wind will result in sorrow (depression, anxiety, a sense of missed opportunities), sickness (ulcers, heart attacks, depression, fatigue...to name a few!) and ultimately anger. Anger at ourselves, anger at our families and anger at God. Ask yourself a few questions:

- Does your present job have you laboring for the wind?
- Are you enduring some of the consequences listed above?

■ What can you do to change the situation?

Sorrow, sickness and anger may be warning signs that you are laboring for the wind. Anxiety and dissatisfaction with work may be God's way of getting you to ask some hard questions. Are you laboring where God wants you to? Are you laboring in the way God wants you to?

But, alas, there is hope. Look at another passage in Ecclesiastes:

> For what has man for all his labor, and for the striving of his heart with which he has toiled under the sun? For all his days are sorrowful, and his work burdensome; even in the night his heart takes no rest. This also is vanity. **Nothing is better for a man than that he should eat and drink, and that his soul should enjoy good in his labor. This also, I saw, was from the hand of God.** *(Ecclesiastes 2:22-24)*

From the last part of the passage we see that not all work is laboring for wind. It is possible for a man to enjoy his labor and glorify God. **Work is not the problem. It is the manner in which we work**.

THE FIRST JOB

Actually, work was God's idea, not ours. In fact, God had the very first job!

And on the seventh day God ended His work which He had done, and He rested on the seventh day from all His work which He had done. *(Genesis 2:2)*

Not only did God have the first job, but He declared that it was good. Part of His work was creating Adam, to whom He gave the world's second job.

Then the LORD God took the man and put him in the garden of Eden to tend and keep it. Out of the ground the LORD God formed every beast of the field and every bird of the air, and brought them to Adam to see what he would call them. And whatever Adam called each living creature, that was its name. *(Genesis 2:15, 19)*

Adam was content and performed his work in perfect fellowship with God until he disobeyed and caused sin to enter the world. With the advent of sin, Adam now had the first work-related blues!

Then to Adam He said, "Because you have heeded the voice of your wife, and have eaten from the tree of which I commanded you, saying, 'You shall not eat of it': "Cursed is the ground for your sake; in toil you shall eat of it all the days of your life. Both thorns and thistles it shall bring forth for you, and you shall eat the herb of the field. In the sweat of your face you shall eat bread till you return to the ground, for out of it you were taken; for dust you are, and to dust you shall return." *(Genesis 3:17-19)*

For years I had used this passage to justify my dissatisfaction with my work. How could I possibly enjoy my work when God had cursed it? Did God not promise that it would be hard and we would hate it? Anyone who said that he enjoyed his work was, in my opinion, either lucky or lying. My goal was just to be obedient and slog through work as best I could, so I could get on to more important spiritual things. With this perspective, it is no wonder that work soon became a drudgery. This same perspective was beginning to cloud other areas of my life as well. But thank God for His Word! In His mercy, He showed me several passages regarding work.

Nothing is better for a man than that he should eat and drink, and **that his soul should enjoy good in his labor**. This also, I saw, was from the hand of God. *(Ecclesiastes 2:24)*

God expects us to enjoy our labor.

I know that nothing is better for them than to rejoice, and to do good in their lives, and

also that every man should eat and drink and **enjoy the good of all his labor — it is the gift of God**. *(Ecclesiastes 3:12-13)*

Work is a gift from God...to be enjoyed!

So I perceived that nothing is better than that a man should **rejoice in his own works, for that is his heritage**. For who can bring him to see what will happen after him? *(Ecclesiastes 3:22)*

Our works will be our heritage. It is what we will be known by. The reformers knew this well. They sought the Lordship of Jesus Christ in every area of their lives. They believed that a man could glorify God just as mightily if he were a cobbler or a clergy. Far from the emphasis being placed on the type of work and how lucrative it is, they concentrated on the manner in which it was performed. God calls each man to a different work, but He requires them to be faithful (emotionally and physically) to that which He has called. What will your "heritage" be? Are you leaving a joyful heritage or a bitter one?

Here is what I have seen: It is good and fitting for one to eat and drink, and to **enjoy the good of all his labor in which he toils under the sun all the days of his life which God gives him;**

for it is his heritage. As for every man to whom God has given riches and wealth, and given him power to eat of it, to receive his heritage and rejoice in his labor — this is the gift of God. **For he will not dwell unduly on the days of his life, because God keeps him busy with the joy of his heart**. *(Ecclesiastes 5:18-20)*

How do we keep from unduly dwelling on our own problems? Enjoy your work and He will keep you busy with the joy of your heart!

So I commended **enjoyment**, because a man has nothing better under the sun than to eat, drink, and be merry; **for this will remain with him in his labor all the days of his life** which God gives him under the sun. *(Ecclesiastes 8:15)*

Solomon did not say that work was bad, only that it could be done badly. What a fool I had been! I had been living under the assumption that only the lucky few could truly enjoy their work. I thought that if I could just bear down and make enough money, I could be free from this wretched thing called work and finally begin enjoying my life. But here was the Scripture totally refuting my world view! Work done in God's manner could be enjoyed.

This changes everything. No more slogging through my workday under the assumption that work stinks and there is nothing to be done about it. No more shoving my work dissatisfaction down deep hoping that it will not break out and spill onto my family and friends. Work is a gift of God to be enjoyed. In fact we are commanded to rejoice in it! So then, why are most Christians dissatisfied with their work? Look at Ecclesiastes 2:24 again.

> Nothing is better for a man than that he should eat and drink, and that his soul should enjoy good in his labor. This also, I saw, **was from the hand of God**.

Job satisfaction comes only from the Lord. You can jump from job to job, and even change careers, and never find contentment if you have not first submitted to the Lordship of Christ in the area of work. He is your Sovereign and He will have no other idols before Him. Submit yourself and your work to Him. Ask Him to show you how to honor Him and follow His priorities in your work. Be willing to change the way in which you work if He so declares. Be willing even to switch jobs or careers if He reveals this to you.

The point of all this is not to find a new job. It is to find a new perspective. Some men need to quit complaining and thank God for the job He has given them. They need to view their job as a gift from God and realize that just as with all gifts from God (sex, music, alcohol, etc.), work must be employed wisely. The type of work is not as important as the manner in which we do it. Perhaps these men need to cut down on the amount of hours in order to be more available for their family. Maybe they need to say "no" to a promotion in order to remain more flexible to disciple younger believers. Whatever career decision we make must be bathed in prayer, keeping God's glory and priorities clearly in the forefront.

Other men may see their careers at cross purposes with godly priorities. Those men need to take a hard look at the Scriptures and make career decisions accordingly. Do not fall into the trap of thinking that the world will take you seriously as a Christian if you are tops in your field. The world begrudgingly honors Christians that are successful, but it is the **success** they honor and not the Christianity! Many Christians have mistakenly given everything they have to their jobs, only to find they have lost their wives and kids in the process. What good are all of the Pulitzer prizes, if you have lost the truly important prizes. "For what profit is it to a man if he gains the whole world, and loses his own soul? Or what will a man give in exchange for his soul?" (Matthew 16:26). Choosing your career over your children is not a biblical option no matter how many accolades the Christian community might heap upon you. And sacrificing your family on the alter of "Christian excellence in the work place" is a lie from the pit! Can I be anymore blunt? **If the reason you are working so hard is to be a witness to the unbelievers at work, while your family suffers from the lack** of your spiritual leadership, you are serving the wrong god! If your teenager is rebelling, God is telling you to pull back from work and take care of the first things first.

While some men may see a glaring problem in the manner they approach work, others may see the growing discontent with their jobs as coming from the Lord. These men should endeavor to see where else the Lord would have them serve. Most men, however, will do nothing. They will not view their relationship with God or the leadership of their families as a high enough priority to warrant action. They will have plenty of Christian friends, and even pastors, who will encourage them not to be rash and to just "pray" until the conviction of the Holy Spirit passes. Even faced with clear direction regarding the priorities of God laid out in His Holy Scriptures, they will choose the easy path of indecision. However, no decision is still a decision and their families will reap again the consequences of this spiritual abdication. I pray that you will not be one of these men. The Christian church, today, has far too many already. If you decide to stay in your present job, then have scriptural reasons for doing so. If through God's leading you decide to change, then choose a job that will give you the flexibility to adequately disciple your children and the young believers God brings your way.

AN ALTERNATIVE

So far we have been exploring ways to glorify God while working in a conventional manner, but there are some alternatives, if you are creative. Consider starting a small family business. What better way to train your children than by having them work alongside you? It does not have to replace your existing job, but who knows where it might lead? As of this date, I am still working full-time as a remodeling contractor, but we have started a curriculum store for home-schoolers that is open two afternoons a week. The children are responsible for unpacking the arriving shipments (checking the contents against the packing slip), finding the code and price on our computer, writing and affixing the appropriate tag on the books, and then placing them on the bookshelf in their appointed place. They help our customers find what they need, check them out on the computer, take their money (making change when paid in cash), and swipe credit cards on the machine. When we travel to book fairs, they are indispensable in packing the books, loading the trailer, unpacking the books, placing them on the shelf, and doing it all over again when it is time to go home. Although it is hard work, they have a blast doing it! They are learning business skills and identifying good books at the same time. More importantly, they are building bonds with us and each other. Bonds that will last a lifetime and have far reaching effects in the generations to come.

Are you ready to think even more outside of the box? Where is it written that we must have only one job or one source of income? In our culture, of course! Multiple sources of income can greatly increase your flexibility. In turn, you can use that flexibility to spend the time it takes to properly train your children to be soldiers for Christ. One of my extra sources of income comes from pulling down old barns. My wife brings the kids out around lunch time and for the rest of the afternoon, they help me pull down boards, pull the nails out and stack the boards on the trailer. While we are working side by side, I teach them biblical principles and how to apply them in today's world. A younger man that I am discipling comes out to help also and I am able to include all three areas at one time...work, ministry and family. Again, the principle here is flexibility. Are you willing to do anything, no matter how unconventional, in order to implement God's priorities? A word of caution is in order. **I am not advocating anything that separates you even more from your kids!** The object of not working in the conventional way is to free up more time to spend with your family. Also, realize that including children in any business will slow you down at first. Having children help run a business is not the most efficient way of doing business, but efficiency is not the goal. The goal is to have a source of income (or incomes) that allows you, under the Lordship of Christ, to dictate how, when and where your income will be made — not someone else with different goals and a different world view. It is an attempt for you to establish godly priorities for yourself and your children.

A FATHER'S STEW

The Third Ingredient: Ministry

SECTION 4

A FATHER'S STEW

THE BIBLICAL VIEW OF MINISTRY

CHAPTER 9

LIVING PURPOSEFULLY

Having read this far, I hope one of the messages that has come through loud and clear is knowing **why you do what you do**. The common thread that weaves through our families, work and ministry should be "living purposefully." It is easy to see the need for this in our families and work. If we do not spend the time and effort required to train our children in godliness, the results are often immediate and tangible. If we are not purposeful in our work, the results are no less immediate and usually affect our pocketbook. But somehow we lose sight of this principle when it comes to ministry. Men who otherwise have very definite ideas on how to glorify God in their families and work, can suddenly get very hazy about what glorifies God in their ministries. What constitutes biblical ministry? After all, we are told, no one has the right to judge what another considers to be his service to God. Attitudes and practices that we would never allow in our homes and work somehow become "okay," if they are done in the name of the Lord. Of course, God knows what true ministry looks like and has revealed this to us in His Word. If there is a single word that best describes the modern evangelical church today, it would be "confusion." We, as a people of God, have no idea where we are headed or how to get there. How else would you explain the foolishness on television where the children of God are exhorted to giggle uncontrollably with holy laughter or perhaps glorify our Lord by barking like a dog? I dare say, that behavior would not fly in your homes or offices!

Why else would our churches portray God as One who primarily meets needs, as opposed to One who saves the ungodly and then, demands their obedience? Why would the fastest growing churches be those that emphasize music and skits over sound biblical teaching? **We have replaced the message with the method.** If "seekers" do not like to hear about a God who will one day judge sin, then we should play down that aspect of His character, in order to "win" more for the kingdom. But we fail to realize that there is no salvation without judgment. We can not have salvation if there is nothing from which to be saved. Are we not being saved from what we justly deserve — the eternal damnation by a just and holy God? Or do you not realize from Whom you are being saved? God the Father sent His Son to save you from **Himself**! I am always amazed when I hear someone say, "Well, my God is a God of love. He would never send anyone to Hell." What god are they describing? It is certainly not the God of the Bible! It is a false god and an idol can never save. We have so little impact on our culture because we have lost our way and have abandoned the purpose for ministry — to bring His children to maturity.

Although confusion characterizes our modern churches, the Son of God was not confused. Robert Coleman gives a wonderful description of Christ's clarity of purpose in his excellent book, The Master Plan of Evangelism.

> *His life was ordered by His objective. Everything He did and said was part of the whole pattern. It had significance because it contributed to the ultimate purpose of His life in redeeming the world for God. This was the motivating vision governing His behavior. His steps were ordered by it. Mark it well. Not for a moment did Jesus lose sight of His goal.*
>
> *That is why it is so important to observe the way Jesus maneuvered to achieve His objective. The Master disclosed God's strategy for world conquest. He had confidence in the future precisely because He lived according to that plan in the present. There was nothing haphazard about His life — no wasted energy, not an idle word. He was on business for God (Luke 2:49). Like a general plotting His course of battle, the Son of God calculated to win.*

The Son of God calculated to win and this is no more apparent than in His prayer in the garden of Gethsemene.

> I have glorified You on the earth. I have finished the work which You have given Me to do. And now, O Father, glorify Me together with Yourself, with the glory which I had with You before the world was. I have manifested Your name to the men whom You have given Me out of the world. They were Yours, You gave them to Me, and they have kept Your word. Now they have known that all things which You have given Me are from You. For I have given to them the words which You have given Me; and they have received them, and have known surely that I came forth from You; and they have believed that You sent Me. *(John 17:4-8)*

Look at Christ's first statement in the preceding passage. Jesus was telling the Father that He had **finished** the work He had been sent to do. Remember this is in the garden of Gethsemene. This was **before** He had gone to the cross to die for the sins of the world! What work is He referring to? His work was to teach the disciples, through His example and the Word, how to glorify the Father. In short, the Father sent the Son to **disciple** twelve men who would, in turn, be able to pass on what they had learned. Please do not misunderstand me. Without Christ's redemptive work on the cross, the disciples would have died in their sins just as we would today. While not taking anything away from Christ's marvelous work on the cross, it is interesting to note the emphasis He places on the training of His men. Look at His priorities concerning them as He continues His prayer.

> I pray for them. I do not pray for the world but for those whom You have given Me, for they are Yours. And all Mine are Yours, and Yours are Mine, and I am glorified in them. *(John 17:9-10)*

Notice who Jesus does **not** pray for. His focus is not on the world, but on the twelve that the Father had given Him. Jesus realized that in order to reach the many, He would have to concentrate on the few. Even among the twelve, Jesus focused on three: Peter, James and John. Our Lord modeled His chosen method for bringing believers to maturity and we would do well to imitate this same method. If our Lord, with all of His resources, found it necessary to pour Himself into a few men at a time, how much more should this principle be followed by His servants. One more point before we leave Jesus' prayer. Duress has a unique ability for sifting out the truly important. Jesus was about to undergo the worst thing imaginable for the Son of God — separation from the Father. This is true for us as well, although we rarely recognize it as such. What was the most pressing thing on Christ's mind before He endured the cross? Was it not the men He had invested His life in? What is the parallel for us? What do we consider the priority in ministry?

Paul had a similar perspective in regards to ministry. Here was a man who knew what God wanted him to do and the method in which to do it. Actually, his situation was not unlike the one most of us have today. He had a full time job and had to carve time out of a very busy schedule, for ministry. He, like us, had limited time and limited resources. And he, like us, had to use that limited time and those limited resources in the most effective way possible. Notice the imagery that Paul uses to describe his life and ministry.

> Do you not know that those who run in a race all run, but one receives the prize? Run in such a way that you may obtain it. And everyone who competes for the prize is temperate in all things. Now they do it to obtain a perishable crown, but we for an imperishable crown. **Therefore I run thus: not with uncertainty. Thus I fight: not as one who beats the air.** But I discipline my body and bring it into subjection, lest, when I have preached to others, I myself should become disqualified. *(1 Corinthians 9:24-27)*

Paul did not run with uncertainty. Nor did he fight as one who throws punches without effect. Given the limitations of time and resources, he knew, that to fulfill his maximum potential for God, he would have to **find God's priorities for ministry and implement them first.** This passage does not convey the image of a man recklessly throwing wild round-house punches, but of someone methodically, unwaveringly, pursuing the goal that God had set before him. Although, the last part of the passage speaks of competing according to the rules, it can also carry the idea of having direction. The runner who aimlessly wanders off the track will be just as disqualified as the one who cheats by taking shortcuts.

So, what was it that Paul was so convinced that God wanted him to do? What was Paul's goal in ministry? As "ministry" has come to mean all sorts of activities that are performed in the name of God, how do we know which ones to choose? How do we know which activities are in accordance with His priorities and will result in maximum glory for Him? Thankfully, He has given the answer in His Word.

> Him we preach, warning every man and teaching every man in all wisdom, that we **may present every man perfect in Christ Jesus.** To this end I also labor, striving according to His working which works in me mightily. *(Colossians 1:28-29)*

Paul was arguably the hardest working Apostle (2 Corinthians 11:23-28) and he clearly gives the reason for all his labor in this passage. Paul's goal was to present every man perfect, or complete, in Christ. Sharing the message of justification was a good start, but he never took his eyes off the ultimate goal — Christian maturity. To this end he labored in God's strength. (Of course, the ultimate goal is to bring glory to God, but the vehicle through which he did this is discipleship.) We see this same idea in the Israelites. While entering the Promised Land was a good start, God's goal for them was to drive out the inhabitants and occupy the land completely. By allowing pockets of resistance to remain, the Israelites were seduced away from their God and fell far short of God's expectations. What an impact they could have had by following God's plan for spiritual maturity! And what about us? Do we become complacent when someone receives the Lord and view anything more in their spiritual life as gravy? Is Christian maturity an unexpected dollop of whip cream on an otherwise complete bowl of salvation? Or, are we striving to bring immature believers to maturity, leaving no pockets of resistance in our churches that may later seduce us away from our God? Are we as vigilant in our own walk? Are we striving for complete Christian maturity in every area of our lives, not settling for mere entrance into the kingdom of God? I am not advocating perfectionism here, for we are all fallen creatures. But one can exercise biblical maturity and wisdom even in a fallen state through Christ's power.

So, we see the necessity for bringing young believers to maturity and yet, we should notice the two things that are working together in the preceding passage. Paul is striving in accordance with God's power. Realizing the source of his effectiveness (God was working in him mightily), he worked like a dog and God gave the increase. Paul worked so hard and with such abandonment, not to satisfy his own agenda, but to satisfy the agenda found in God's Word. Notice what Paul did not consider the goal of his ministry:

- To get more people into church
  Numbers do not equate to lasting impact. Five well trained commandos can be more effective than one-hundred raw recruits.

- To lose himself in ever increasingly emotional worship services
  Our purpose is to present every man complete in Christ, not to manipulate emotions at the expense of true worship; which is in spirit and truth (John 4:24).

- To meet the needs of ever increasing "special interest" groups
  Although we should recognize the diversity of the body of Christ, the goal of the church is not to separate and divide. We should be careful not dichotomize the church into separate entities which can fester and produce malcontent. Youth groups, widows groups, groups for the elderly, divorce groups, children of alcoholic parents groups, substance abuse groups, etc. The list goes on and on.

- To gain unity at the expense of doctrine
  Those who do not hold to the deity of Christ have no place in our pulpits, whether as guest speakers or otherwise. Organizations that promote "Christian" unity while setting aside the revealed truths of the Word of God, are blasphemous and damage credibility with the unbelieving world.

- To be culturally relevant
  If a culture rejects God, how can we imitate it without becoming like it? Yes, we have many life experiences in common with unbelievers and we should use them to develop relationships, but we are primarily called to be set apart. Instead of trying to bring God's truth down to their level, let us raise up the gospel of truth and allow the attractiveness of His holiness to draw men unto Himself.

JUDGMENT BEGINS WITH US

The fact that Paul's goals for ministry are so radically different from the goals of the modern evangelical church should alarm us. In fact, our goals seem to be more in line with the carnal church at Corinth. 1 Peter 4:17 makes it clear that judgment will start with the house of God. If our churches desire any significant impact on the world, we must fall on our knees and repent for having adulterous priorities. We must look to God's Word to identify His priorities and implement them first.

> My people are destroyed for lack of knowledge. Because you have rejected knowledge, I also will reject you from being priest for Me; Because you have forgotten the law of your God, I also will forget your children. *(Hosea 4:6)*

Here God is attacking the "why can't we forget about doctrine and just learn to love one another" crowd. When we ignore Scripture or down-play its importance in our churches, we are inviting God to reject us and ignore our children. God's work must be run God's way. The only way to determine what true ministry is and the manner in which it should be executed is to search the Scriptures. This is one area that we can not "make it up as we go."

As I said before, God's judgment will start with the house of God. Doug Wilson makes the interesting observation that homosexuality, disobedient children and feminism in our nation and churches not only invite judgment, they are a sign of the judgment that is **already here**! These three in particular have always been a sign that God has judged His people and is calling them to repentance.

> Woe to the wicked! It shall be ill with him,
> For the reward of his hands shall be given him.
> As for My people, **children are their oppressors,**
> **And women rule over them**.

O My people! Those who lead you cause
you to err,
And destroy the way of your paths.
(Isaiah 3:11-12)

Read Lamentation chapter 4 to see how severely God will deal with **His own people** when necessary. If judgment is already upon the house of God, what can we do about it? How can we get back to the point where we stumbled off the path?

You, O LORD, remain forever;
Your throne from generation to generation.
Why do You forget us forever,
And forsake us for so long a time?
Turn us back to You, O LORD, and we will
be restored;
Renew our days as of old,
Unless You have utterly rejected us,
And are very angry with us!
(Lamentations 5:19-22)

The passage above provides both hope and a stern warning. **First, judgment on the people of God can last a long time.** God did not chastise His people for a few months and then relent. The Israelites were in captivity for seventy years before they were allowed to go home and even then they were under the authority of an oppressive ungodly regime. God may grant mercy and renew us to the days of old, but we must face the possibility that we are beyond the point of return. The modern evangelical church has made God very angry with its polytheism (many roads to heaven), materialistic idolatry, deplorable lack of holiness and disregard for His commands that we find unfair or inconvenient. We must do as our forefathers did and cry out to our God in repentance. Perhaps He will listen and not break off the wild olive branch that has been grafted in (Romans 11:19-21).

A FATHER'S STEW

CHAPTER 10

ATTAINING THE GOAL OF MINISTRY

CHRISTIAN MATURITY

If the goal in ministry is to bring every Christian to spiritual maturity, then we need to know what spiritual maturity is. It is hard to build a house if we do not know what the final structure should look like when we are finished building. Again, Scripture gives us the answer to our dilemma.

> But solid food belongs to those who are of full age, that is, **those who by reason of use have their senses exercised to discern both good and evil**. Therefore, leaving the discussion of the elementary principles of Christ, let us go on to perfection, not laying again the foundation of repentance from dead works and of faith toward God, of the doctrine of baptisms, of laying on of hands, of resurrection of the dead, and of

eternal judgment. **And this we will do if God permits**. *(Hebrews 5:14-6:3)*

Notice what the writer of Hebrews was calling the elementary principles of Christ: repentance, faith, baptism, laying on of hands, the resurrection and eternal judgment. Most pastors would turn cartwheels if their congregations knew even this much! But the author of Hebrews was not content to settling for the basics. He goes on to describe the process of spiritual maturity to his readers. As a man engages the Scriptures and begins to put those concepts to use in his daily affairs, he develops his senses to the point where he can discern good and evil. This discernment is not just the rudimentary identification of obvious sin. It is the sophistication to aptly identify certain sins under the layers of good intentions. It is the ability to not only point out a wrong, but to identify where, along the process, sin crept into our thinking which led to the wrong in the first place.

This type of discernment does not come from a cursory reading of Scripture or from most of the drivel you find on the shelves of Christian book stores today. It comes from the diligent reading of the Word, reading of excellent Christian material and the disciplined application of that which has been learned. From the last verse in the preceding passage, we see that spiritual maturity is very much a God-ordained activity. Men will come to maturity **only** if God permits. No true maturity can occur apart from God's sovereign hand. It can not be manufactured by human efforts or packaged in some ten-step church program. It falls from on high and He gets the glory.

> I planted, Apollos watered, but God gave the increase. So then neither he who plants is anything, nor he who waters, but God who gives the increase. *(1 Corinthians 3:6-7)*

Although we are sinful creatures and will never attain perfection this side of heaven, we can say that a man is mature if he meets certain criteria. What things should we look for when the "house" is finished? What characteristics do we want our "Timothy" to exhibit when we are finished building in him? Below is a list to at least get us started.

- He can study the Word on his own.
- He is grounded in basic doctrine.
- He has a consistent quiet time.
- He has a consistent prayer life.
- He has fellowship with other believers.
- He is dealing with known sin in his life.
- He has godly priorities.
- He has visible fruit in his life.
- He can share his faith with non believers.
- He is serving the body in some capacity.
- He is reproducing himself in another person.

The last characteristic may not be as obvious. Remember your high school biology class? When do we call a plant or animal "mature?" A dog can reach its full size in a year, but we do not consider it mature until it is capable of reproduction. To extend the analogy further, we would think there was a problem if the dog, under normal circumstances, could not reproduce. Similarly, we know something is wrong in our churches when "mature" believers are not reproducing themselves in others. One of the characteristics of true spiritual maturity is the ability to reproduce oneself in another believer.

GOD'S METHOD FOR MATURITY

But how did Paul present every man complete or mature in Christ? What was his God-ordained method for accomplishing this goal?

> And the things that you have heard from me among many witnesses, **commit these to faithful men who will be able to teach others also**. *(2 Timothy 2:2)*

Paul wrote Second Timothy while imprisoned and knew that his death was near. Knowing this would be your last letter to your most faithful student, what would you want to communicate? Would it not be those things that are most essential? Would you not charge him with the most important of duties? Paul charged Timothy to commit God's

truths, not only to faithful men, but to those who would in turn, commit them to others also. Paul impressed on Timothy to not just make disciples, but to make **disciple-makers**. It was not enough to teach men the truths of God. They had to be taught in such a way that they could teach others as well. This principle is also seen in our Lord's last commandment given to His disciples.

> And Jesus came and spoke to them, saying, "All authority has been given to Me in heaven and on earth. Go therefore and make disciples of all the nations, baptizing them in the name of the Father and of the Son and of the Holy Spirit, teaching them to observe all things that I have commanded you; and lo, I am with you always, even to the end of the age." *(Matthew 28:18-20)*

If you were leaving loved ones for a long time, would you tell them all of the **trivial** things you wanted them to remember? No, you would concentrate on the most important. The things not to be missed! Jesus knew He would be gone for a long time after His resurrection. In fact, He would be gone long past His disciples' life times. He left them with the most important of all duties. The duty to make disciples.

One of the main lessons we learn from history is that ideas have consequences. This is why it is essential to have correct doctrine. Having an incorrect understanding of doctrine will lead to an incorrect understanding of the world, which will inevitably result in unbiblical decisions and behaviors. Nowhere is this more evident than in our understanding of the Apostles. Most of us have the notion that the Apostles wandered around with Jesus bumbling through life, occasionally getting things right, but for the most part, making one mistake after another. Only until Pentecost did the Apostles finally get "zapped" with supernatural power and then became the wise men who could boldly refute the best theologians of their day. One could surmise that the entire three and a half years spent with Jesus were in vain. Why would Jesus spend all that time and energy when He had only to send the Holy Spirit, and "Shazam," achieve instant maturity? Again, we think in these terms, because we do not understand the doctrine of discipleship. There would not have been a Pentecost if the Apostles had not been properly trained beforehand. Jesus spent three and half long years filling the reservoir from which the Apostles drew for the rest of their lives. Pentecost was the spark which ignited the carefully laid wood to produce a lasting fire. We live in an age of instant coffee and instant oatmeal. The kind of lifestyle it took our parents fifty years to obtain, young families want now. If it takes more than a few years to see the results, it is not worth doing. With this mentality, it is no wonder that most Christians do not have the patience nor the will to obtain biblical maturity for themselves, much less lead others to it.

OUR MODERN CHURCHES VS. SPIRITUAL MATURITY

But most churches have a discipleship program. Some churches have even hired a discipleship pastor. Why then do so few Christians achieve the true spiritual maturity described in Hebrews and elsewhere in the Bible? Why then do so many Christian churches make such little impact in their communities? Perhaps the answer lies in our perception of the church's function. When we as evangelicals, view this world as a sinking ship, then the main goal becomes getting people into the lifeboats. Scrambling for the lifeboats does not leave a lot of time for leading young Christians to maturity. In fact, we are not sure what to do with them once we get them there. Usually, we are praying they will not tip the silly things over! "Do as you are told, don't make waves and you will be okay."

I can illustrate this mentality by asking a simple question. If you were to ask most evangelicals today who this earth belongs to, what would be their first response? They will undoubtedly say the Devil. But Scripture teaches that "the earth is the Lord's and all its fullness" (1 Corinthians 10:26 and Exodus 9:29). The earth belongs to the Lord Jesus Christ and He has given us a mandate to be fruitful, multiply and subdue the earth. This mandate was first given to Adam and was reiterated to Noah after the flood. This means it is still in effect for us, today. We are to subdue this earth for its rightful owner, the Lord Jesus Christ. If evangelical Christians are confused as to Who is in control, how can we ever hope to win the battle? Far from simply getting people into lifeboats, we are to train believers to be soldiers who can cross enemy lines, conquer territory and bring back captives. And those captives are to be trained in such a way that they in turn can charge across enemy lines, conquer even more territory and bring back even more captives. Of course all of this is done in God's power, for He is sovereign and He gets the glory.

A great illustration of man's work in concert with God's sovereignty is found in Proverbs.

> **The horse is prepared for the day of battle, but deliverance is of the LORD.** *(Proverbs 21:31)*

Anyone who has worked with horses can tell you how hard it is to overcome their natural instinct to flight. A sudden move or strange sound can send a horse into a panicked retreat. In light of this, how hard do you think it would be to make a horse run headlong into thousands of screaming men swinging battle axes? I wager it would take years of daily training to prepare that horse for battle and yet, where does Scripture tell us the deliverance comes from? When the training and the fighting are over, it is the One who determines the outcome that receives the glory.

While some churches view their function as packing sinners into lifeboats (which may be the reason they spend so much energy building bigger and more luxurious lifeboats), other churches view their calling similar to that of hospitals. Far from training soldiers, their mission is to be a safe haven for the battered and bruised. While I will grant you that even an army has a MASH tent to treat those who have been wounded in battle, the expectation is for them to heal and rejoin the fight. If we train our men only to counsel, listen to hurts and to be sensitive, will this training win the war or cause more casualties? Men who enter battle knowing only how to comfort and not how to fight will endanger themselves and those around them. Toughness and, dare I say it, a certain degree of insensitivity are desirable characteristics for soldiers.

One of the principles we learn from studying military campaigns is that if the enemy kills a man on the battlefield, he will take one man out of the fight. If he wounds a man, he will take three men out of the fight — the one wounded and his two buddies who have to carry him to safety (who, now, are at a greater risk of being wounded themselves). Our enemy, Satan, knows this principle very well and has used it to great effect on the church of God. Satan can create more havoc by **wounding** a Christian than by taking him out completely. And when we view our churches primarily as long term care for the hurting and wounded, we are only playing into his hand. At the risk of sounding insensitive, which is more cruel? Should we enable hurting Christians to stay in their present state or come alongside, as James exhorts, and bring these hurting ones to the point of understanding and repentance? This will lead to **true** liberty in Christ (James 5:19-20).

This may sound like church-bashing, but in reality I am calling the church to repentance. Christ reserved some harsh words for the Church at Ephesus.

> I know your works, your labor, your patience, and that you cannot bear those who are evil. And you have tested those who say they are apostles and are not, and have found them liars; and you have persevered and have patience, and have labored for My name's sake and have not become weary. Nevertheless I have this against you, that you have left your first love. Remember therefore from where you have fallen; **repent and do the first works**, or else I will come to you quickly and remove your lampstand from its place — **unless you repent**. *(Revelation 2:2-5)*

This church had a lot going for it. They labored, removed those who were evil, and tested false teachers by the Word of God. By most accounts, this would be a stellar church worthy of praise and recognition. But they had a small problem. They had left their first love. How do we know this? Was their worship service not dynamic enough? Did they not quiver with enough excitement when they met on Sunday morning? Were they not culturally relevant enough for the spiritually curious that came on Sunday morning? No, Scripture states that they had stopped doing their first

works. What were the first works? Well, the Great Commission would be a good place to start. And the Greatest Commandment would be another. The Great Commission expressly tells us to disciple other believers (which would include our children, of course) and the Greatest Commandment expressly tells us to love God with the resulting action of training our children to do the same (Deuteronomy 6:4-7). Both of these first works involve discipleship. Unless we repent and make it a priority in our churches to disciple our children and younger believers, the preceding passage in Revelation makes the consequence very plain. God will take away what little light we have left. Make no mistake. He has already severely judged our modern evangelical churches and unless we repent, remember from where we have fallen, and begin to do the first things, He will give our job to another just as He did with Israel.

One of the greatest gifts we have lost in modern times is that of a multi-generational view. If it can not be done in our life times, it is not worth doing. But just a few years ago, there were men and women who left everything to start a new life in a foreign land and give their children the opportunity to worship God unfettered by corrupt church leaders and government officials. These were men and women who viewed their own lives as stepping stones for their children and their children's children. They were able to endure immense hardship and danger because of their conviction that God is a God who visits blessings to the thousandth generation of those who love him and keep His commandments (Deuteronomy 7:9-11).

They were, of course, our forefathers who founded this country. Are we willing to make the same sacrifice for our children and our children's children? Are we willing to forego temporal pleasures and a standard of living to ensure that our children are trained in godliness? Are we willing to "pour ourselves out as a drink offering" to ensure the maturity and depth of believers in our local church?

I must give a qualifier here, with the knowledge that it will offend some. You may be wondering why I use the term "ministry" as an ingredient to our stew when I have primarily written about discipleship. The reason is simple. There is no true ministry without discipleship. Anything a church is involved in must be a supplement to the main goal — that of bringing all its members to full maturity in Christ. On the flip side, any activity that impedes, entangles or interferes with the leading of its members to maturity in Christ should be abolished immediately. Remember the example of busyness in our families? The same is true of our churches. Busyness is the mortal enemy of church discipleship. May I take this one step further? If your only ministry is playing music in the church, you do not have biblical priorities. Music is a wonderful supplement, but your main priority, according to the Word of God, is to "present every man complete in Christ." Again, if your only "ministry" is to pass the plate on Sunday, you have sold your inheritance for a mess of pottage (Hebrews 12:14-17).

THE NECESSITY
CHAPTER 11 OF DISCIPLESHIP

HAND-TO-HAND COMBAT

We are a nation who clamors for instant results and nowhere is this more apparent than in our churches. We offer a **six-week** discipleship course designed to bring the new Christian up to full speed, as if that were enough time to get the job done. Most churches do not even have this and new believers are lucky if they have an orientation lasting two Sundays after they have joined the church. "But, we have a wonderful pastor who preaches the Word faithfully. Won't the new believers come to maturity through this?" A pastor can preach a strong, convicting message from the pulpit and most will go away thinking about others who should have heard the message. It is an altogether different matter to sit across the table from a man, guiding him in the Word, and then asking him how he is applying those truths in his day to day life. Perhaps an illustration would help. World War II and the many wars that have followed have proven that we can not conquer a nation by conventional bombing. There are just too many places for the enemy to hide. Foreign soil has to be taken city by city and house by house. Even with the most technologically advanced smart bombs and guided missiles, the infantry is still required to take and hold territory. Similarly, we can not lob Scripture from afar at new believers in our churches. We must take the fight to them and engage in hand to hand combat for the maturity of young believers. This same principle is required for unbelievers as well. We can not bring unbelievers to church so the "professional hired gun" (pastor) can win them for Jesus. We must train the believers in our churches to be able to articulate the gospel to their unbelieving friends and then, bring them to maturity in Christ.

That is why church programs will not get the job done. A program is not equipped to cut through the layers of defensiveness and ignorance that plague our new believers today. Remember the woman at the well? No amount of literature, stirring messages or church programs would have brought her to saving belief. She had too many smoke screens and red herrings. Someone had to engage her personally, parry every counter argument and answer her questions, while relentlessly bringing her back to the main issue. Am I saying that we should not have pastors or preaching from the pulpit? Certainly not! I am saying, however, that there is no substitute for a mature believer pouring his life into another believer and this is God's revealed design for bringing the church to maturity. Above all, we are not to fall into the trap of modern efficiency. "If one on one is good, then one on thirty is better. Better yet, why not tape a discipleship program and play it to an auditorium full of people. Or a stadium. Both Christ and Paul modeled discipleship as an intensely personal endeavor.

Perhaps this is best illustrated by a quote from another good book on discipleship entitled <u>The Lost Art of Disciple Making</u> by Leroy Eims.

> During one of our moves we bought a new house that had no lawn; the front and back yards were just bare earth. A friend of ours bought some sod for us, and at the same time our neighbor bought his sod from the same company. When they were both laid they looked beautiful (so much so that the landscaping company used our two lawns in some of their promotional advertising).
>
> Our neighbor decided to water his lawn with an automatic underground sprinkler system, which he had installed before the lawn was laid. I chose to buy a hose and turn it over to my wife, Virginia. So I had a blonde out there with a hose watering my lawn while my neighbor would merely turn his controls on and off.
>
> After four years my neighbor's lawn returned to its original state — just bare earth covered

with weeds. Our lawn was still green and beautiful. What made the difference? Personal care. Whenever Virginia would see a brown spot on the grass, she would give it special attention and more water. With the mechanical system there was no way to give individual care and attention to the grass; as holes in the sprinklers were clogged by dirt and small stones, certain portions of the lawn received no water. Soon the lawn dried up and was destroyed, while ours remained lush and green.

You cannot turn over a lawn to a mechanical system in a dry climate such as ours and expect success. Each blade of grass needs special care. That is much more true with people. Each of us has specific needs and these can only be met by other people. No system or program will automatically meet and cure the needs of human beings. Because we are individuals, we have specific needs which people alone can meet.

Another mistake to avoid is what I call the buffet approach to spiritual maturity. Just because a church makes good material available to its members for spiritual growth, does not mean the members will use it. What if I took my children to a buffet and found them loading their plates from the dessert end of the food bar, while having nothing nutritious from the other end? I would not be much of a father if I said, "At least I have given them the opportunity to eat a nutritious meal, even if they choose not to!" Immature believers are naturally immature. By definition, they will not naturally gravitate towards things that cause temporary discomfort or require self-control. We need to come alongside and help them choose items that contribute to a well-balanced meal. We need to encourage and even rebuke when they try to pile on their plates things that do harm to themselves and to others. Above all, we need to teach them how to feed themselves and eventually, teach others to do the same. As leaders and elders, we must be shepherds and not merely administrators.

THE PRICE FOR NOT DISCIPLING OTHERS

At the risk of beating a dead horse, may I give one final encouragement to be involved in the leading of men and women to true maturity in Christ?

> For we are God's fellow workers; you are God's field, you are God's building. According to the grace of God which was given to me, as a wise master builder I have laid the foundation, and another builds on it. But let each one take heed how he builds on it. For no other foundation can anyone lay than that which is laid, which is

Jesus Christ. Now if anyone builds on this foundation with gold, silver, precious stones, wood, hay, straw, each one's work will become clear; for the Day will declare it, because it will be revealed by fire; and the fire will test each one's work, of what sort it is. If anyone's work which he has built on it endures, he will receive a reward. If anyone's work is burned, he will suffer loss; but he himself will be saved, yet so as through fire. *(1 Corinthians 3:9-15)*

To understand this passage, it is imperative that we understand who is doing what. Paul is describing himself as a wise master builder and the Corinthians are his building. He laid the foundation, which is Jesus Christ, but there are others who are continuing to build on the Corinthians. I had always taken this passage as a warning to be careful how I build into myself. But the context indicates that Paul is warning others to be careful how they build into other men. In fact, we will be judged at the Judgment Seat of Christ as to how we have built into other men's lives. We should be building in such a way, and using such material, that our work will endure God's purifying fire, for then we will receive a reward. Can this passage have more than one meaning? Could it be describing our own sanctification as well as our involvement in another's sanctification? Most certainly. But if you come to the Judgment Seat of Christ and you are missing one of the main criteria by which you will be judged (building in other men's lives), then you will not experience a very pleasant judgment and it is doubtful you will hear, "Well done good and faithful servant" (Matthew 25:23).

SHORE UP THE HOME FRONT

Now is the time for battle. But before you go out to fight, make sure you have properly prepared your defenses at home, lest the enemy find a weakness while you are away at battle. Our first priority, as fathers, should be to disciple our wives and children. In fact, 2 Timothy 3:5 tells us that a man who can not rule his own house has no business running the house of God. Although this is in the context of elders and church leadership, the principle still applies to discipleship. How can you export what you do not have? If your children are disobedient or ignorant of the Scriptures, follow God's priorities and deal with them first.

Having said this, I am not espousing neglecting disciple-making until after your kids have grown and left the house. One of the best ways to disciple your own kids is to let them see you disciple younger believers. Having seen your ministry first hand, they will assume this is normative behavior and will be more likely to follow the pattern you have set. However, we must remember the order of God's priorities. We have no business discipling other men unless we have first begun to disciple our children. If you can not afford the time to train your children **and** other men, then your children take top priority.

A FATHER'S STEW

HOW TO DISCIPLE ANOTHER

CHAPTER 12

WHAT KIND OF SHOES?

Hopefully, I have persuaded you of the importance of leading a fellow believer to maturity. I have not meant to discount the leading of an unbeliever to Christ. How marvelous! Not only have you been used by God to change his eternal destiny, but now you have a ready soul waiting to be led to maturity. This is before other believers have convinced him that maturity is too hard or unattainable in this life. I must also reiterate that unless the Lord builds a house, they that build it labor in vain (Psalms 127:1). We can not bring a man to maturity in our own strength. Only reliance on His power and adherence to His methods will grant success. That is why Robert Coleman's book, <u>The Master Plan of Evangelism</u>, is so effective. It chronicles how the **Master** discipled the twelve. And who can argue with the results? Twelve men who turned the world upside down and were faithful even to the death.

But how do we lead a man to maturity? Where do we start? I suggest we start by asking the question that any manufacturer would ask before he starts the machinery. What are you trying to produce? If you were making shoes, you would at least like to know that the items coming out of the other end of the assembly line were in actuality, shoes! In fact, you would probably have a model shoe or prototype to ensure that you faithfully produce what you are intending to produce. Thankfully, we have the Word of God to guide us. We look to the Scriptures to see what God considers a mature man and then work towards that goal. Earlier, I included a list of characteristics that a mature man should have, according to the Bible. Let us look at the list again with the purpose of seeing what the end product should look like.

- He can study the Word on his own.

- He is grounded in basic doctrine.

- He has a consistent quiet time.

- He has a consistent prayer life.

- He has fellowship with other believers.

- He is dealing with known sin in his life.

- He has godly priorities.

- He has visible fruit in his life.

- He can share his faith with non believers.

- He is serving the body in some capacity.

- He is reproducing himself in another person.

Some of the men God will bring to you will be very new believers. They will have very few of these characteristics. Our job will be to get them into the Word as soon as possible and give them lots of basic instruction. They will pepper you with hundreds of questions and will have lots of "carry-over" from their old life, but do not despair. Many times these new believers are very eager to study the Word of God and just as eager to apply what they have learned. Although it can be very draining, it can also be very refreshing working with a clean slate. You will not have to dismantle a lot of bad understanding about God because they will not know very much to begin with.

Others will be further along in their understanding and may only need encouragement in a few areas. Many believers know a fair amount of doctrine (although I have found that when challenged, they know less than they thought), but lack God's power in their lives. They are inconsistent in their quiet times and have dismal prayer lives. They may have led others to Christ, but are unsure what to do with them after that. They bring their new converts to church and watch helplessly as these converts fail to grow and finally, either fall between the cracks or settle into a mediocre Christian lifestyle. Our job will be to encourage these men to come alongside their new converts to bring them to maturity and then give them the tools to do it. Even if you get a man who seems to have everything going well in his walk with the Lord, do not skip over the fundamentals. You never know what he may be missing in his knowledge of God and besides, he will soon have to articulate the fundamentals to his "Timothy" anyway.

Now that we have an idea of the characteristics we are trying to produce in our disciple, we can now list some biblical topics we will need to cover. Remember, we are filling a reservoir that he can tap into as he makes life decisions and brings others to maturity in Christ.

- Salvation
  He needs to know the gospel backwards and forwards.

- Assurance of Salvation
  If God has chosen us from the foundation of the world, how can He lose us?

- Discipleship
  The cost, the resources, the plan, the hazards and the rewards.

- The Word of God
  It's origin, authority, inerrancy, study methods, memorization and meditation. Our response.

- Characteristics of God
  His omniscience, omnipotence and omnipresence. Also, His holiness, infinitude and sovereignty.

- Jesus Christ
  His deity, humanity, work on the cross and coming judgment.

- Fellowship with God
  Quiet time, prayer, confession, worship and obedience.

- Fellowship with Family
  The role of the husband and wife in marriage and raising godly children.

- Fellowship with Other Believers
  Love, fellowship, resolving conflicts, unity and church discipline.

- Our Resources in Christ
  New creation, old sin nature, the Holy Spirit, rewards and victory over sin.

- The Lordship of Christ
  Time management, godly priorities, godly perspective, lifestyle choices, family relationships, personal behavior and knowing the will of God.

- Serving God
  Giving, spiritual gifts and church structure.

- Spiritual Warfare
  Satan, end times, witnessing and making disciple-makers.

LAY YOUR CARDS ON THE TABLE

Before I consent to disciple a man, I spend a lot of time in prayer over him. Again, this is spiritual warfare. Jesus spent time praying before He chose His men (Luke 6:12-13) and He knew them before He created the world! If the Master felt the necessity for prayer beforehand, how much more the servant? However, you must realize that not everyone is ready to be discipled. While I will assert that discipleship is God's chosen method for bringing younger believers to maturity, it may take a while to convince the church of this. Just as an unbeliever must sometimes be brought around slowly to the claims of the gospel (ie: many nights of answering questions and lots of love demonstrated through actions), so a new believer may not see the need for deep personal discipleship right away. Some loaves of bread are just not ready to pull out of the oven. They need a little more time. Trying to work with them prematurely will only result in frustration for both the discipler and disciplee. Unfortunately, some loaves will never be ready and a wise man will better spend his time with those that are.

Other young believers will be only too happy to spend time with you. They will see your life and be attracted by your spiritual maturity. They may have even heard that you spend time regularly with younger believers. When you approach them to join a discipleship group, they will readily accept. But unless you are very precise about your goals and expectations, you may both be in for a major disappointment. Why? Because even though you and your disciple will hold each other accountable to the Word of God, it is not an accountability group. Although you may experience intense fellowship, it is not the forever fellow-

ship club. And though Scripture will be fundamental to what you are doing, it is not the eternal Bible study. All three of these things are essential ingredients, but discipleship is so much more! You are not merely making disciples or followers of Christ, you are making **disciple-makers**. Men, who after spending time with you, will be equipped to do the same with others that God brings into their lives. Faithful man who, as Paul writes to Timothy, "will be able to teach others also." There will be many pressures and temptations to alter the goal of the group, but do not succumb. This is why I always put a time limit with every man or group I work with. When that time limit is reached, I fully expect to disband the group, pair up with one of the members in the group and start another group. No one is allowed to join the group without the full expectation that they will take on a "Timothy" or be an assistant to someone else who takes on a "Timothy."

HOW I HAVE DONE IT

I have discipled men in various ways. By far the easiest way is one-on-one. It is relatively simple to choose a time acceptable for the two of us (as opposed to five or six) and there is less chance of him being a "no show" without a good reason. We meet once a week for about two hours. We usually spend the first hour catching up on what God has done in our lives during the past week, writing down prayer requests, praying and asking about each other's daily time with the Lord. We then spend about an hour going through a lesson that was given to them the previous week and which covers one of the biblical topics found in the list given earlier in this chapter. Not being able to find a canned approach to discipleship that I liked, I have written my own discipleship materials that start off with real-life scenarios with applicable verses to study. I intentionally give them hard questions in the scenarios and relatively few verses to start with, because I want them to learn to dig into the Scriptures for themselves.

If you are interested in the curriculum that I have written and use, it is titled Teaching Faithful Men to Teach Others Also: Making Disciple-Makers. If you are working with a man who knows very little or who is a new believer, you may want to use another curriculum that I have written, Foundations: A Bible Study for the New Believer. These books are available at Ranger Press, an imprint of Morgan James Publishing. After about ten lessons with my curriculum, we will read Robert Coleman's The Master Plan of Evangelism and then Douglas Wilson's Reforming Marriage. Even if you are discipling college kids, they need to be taught the biblical principles of marriage which they will probably not hear in your average college Sunday school class. Besides, what better time to know about marriage than **before they are actually married**.

Another way I have discipled men is two on two. I will take a man that I have just spent a year with (going through the ten lessons and the two books mentioned above), and will pair up with two other young believers. He will serve as my assistant and perhaps lead the first hour, while I lead the teaching time in the second hour. Over time, I will work him into teaching the second hour as he gains confidence. At the end of the discipleship time, my assistant will take one of the new believers and find two more new believers. He will use the one who has just been through the material as his assistant. I will grab the other new believer as my new assistant and we will find two other young believers. The beauty of this method is that a man has been through the material **twice** under another's tutelage before attempting to do it on his own. One warning, however. Finding a time that four men can meet (especially college students) can be a daunting task. It may be easier for a camel to go through the eye of a needle!

The last method I have used to disciple men has had mixed results. I invite whoever wants to come to a discipleship group and lay down the rules once they are there. The problem is lack of control. Men will come to your discipleship group for many reasons and they may not all be on the same page, in regards to the commitment of making disciple-makers. And once you have ten guys coming regularly to a discipleship group, are you going to disband it when you have covered your lessons and books? What do you do with the young believers that are coming and getting a lot out of the Bible study, but are not ready or mature enough to grab a "Timothy" of their own? I have learned to relax about these groups and select one or two men out of them to go deeper with. These type of

Bible studies have become my fishing pond to see who rises to the surface for more intense training. One of the main problems with this approach is kicking men out of the nest. The Bible study is very comfortable and feels very spiritual. If they do not have time to attend this Bible study **and** disciple a new believer, they will be more likely to choose the Bible study only. You may unwittingly create the eternal Bible study and siphon away precious energy from disciple-making. Your only recourse is to continually reiterate the goal of making disciple-makers. Remind them again and again what the true priority is.

Although there are many methods to disciple young believers, the underlying principles are the same and have been since God first instituted them in the Garden of Eden. It was Adam, after all, who was responsible to teach Eve concerning the Tree of the Knowledge of Good and Evil. First, concentrate on a few. One of the recurring themes in Robert Coleman's The Master Plan of Evangelism is that of concentrating on the few in order to reach the many. We have already looked at Christ's prayer in the garden of Gethsemene. He did not pray for the world, but for the few that God had given Him, specifically the twelve. Even within the twelve, Jesus gave extra time to the three. We would do well to follow His example and in so doing, we will have churches that are more than a "mile wide and an inch thick." Second, identify from Scripture what you want your man to look like and then build accordingly. Third, communicate the goal of making disciple-makers early and often.

A FATHER'S STEW

And remember that disciple-making is a universal activity. It is something you can do in any country, any time of your life and in any profession you choose. Not only is it rewarding and makes our joy complete, but it is God's prescribed method for bringing His children to maturity. Above all, it is something we are commanded to do by our Lord and King.

A FATHER'S STEW

EPILOGUE

Well, there you have it. How to biblically integrate our families, work and ministry in three easy steps! Hardly. It is perhaps the most difficult thing a man can set out to do. After all, King David conquered a country, but could not rule his own sons. Yet, to this task we are called and will one day be held accountable. Will we be men who cry out to God for His mercy and strength to skillfully blend these essential areas of our lives? Or will we follow the path of the world (and unfortunately, the modern day church) — handing our children, work, and ministries over to professionals who may be more qualified on paper, but lack the shepherding instinct of those who care for their own. Hopefully we will be like Joshua and tell the world; you can do what you want, but as for me and my house, we will serve the Lord.

During the heyday of the Monica Lewinsky scandal, a reporter asked President Clinton's press secretary how the President was able to deal with the scandal and still ably lead our country. The press secretary thought for a moment and then remarked, "The President has great powers of compartmentalization." That is the world's way of saying that we can **separate** our personal and professional lives. I would submit that President Clinton was **not** able to "deal" with the scandal and still do his job well — and neither can we. Our lives are like a stew with work, family and ministry being the ingredients. Each brings a different characteristic, but all combine to form one flavor. Too much of one thing or not enough of the other, can knock the stew out of balance and produce an offensive taste for us as well as others. When we have problems at home, it will not be long before they surface at the office. Similarly, we can not have problems at the office and be terribly surprised when they begin to follow us home. Problems in our family and work will eventually affect our ministry and if the problems are severe enough, will disqualify us for ministry altogether. If we have no ministry (ie: not actively involved in one another's lives), then how will our children ever learn to serve the Lord? You see, it is all intertwined. God never intended for us to divide our life into separate entities over which we have sovereign control. He is the Lord over all areas in our lives and He is the One to Whom we must give an accounting.

You see, I have a dream. My dream is that my work can bless my kids and not rob from them. That my kids can help me in my work and I would be willing to share it with them. That my kids will see me and my wife discipling young believers and that these young believers will see the way we raise our children, and both will be blessed by what they see. That my work can include some of my disciples so I can spend more time with them and, in turn, they would be willing to help me in my work. My prayer is that that **all** areas of my life be brought under subjection to Him and that as a stew, it would be a sweet-smelling aroma, an acceptable sacrifice, well pleasing to God (Philippians 4:18).

A FATHER'S STEW

 # RESOURCES

Covenantal Discipline, Audio, Matt Whitling, Canon Press, 2000

Excused Absence: Should Christian Kids Leave Public Schools?, Douglas Wilson, Crux Press, 2001

The Heart of Anger, Lou Priolo, Cavalry Press, 1998

The Law, Fredric Bastiat, The Foundation for Economics Education, 1998

The Lost Art of Disciple Making, Leroy Eims, Zondervan Publishing House, 1978

The Master Plan of Evangelism, Robert E. Coleman, New Spire, 2000

No Greater Joy (Volumes 1-3), Michael Pearl, Church at Cane Creek, 1997, 1999, 2000

The Paideia of God, Douglas Wilson, Canon Press, 1999

Reforming Marriage, Douglas Wilson, Canon Press, 1995

To Train Up A Child, Michael Pearl, Church at Cane Creek, 2000

CLAIM YOUR FREE BONUS IMMEDIATELY

WWW.RANGERPRESS.COM/STEW.HTM

Now that you are aware of these life-changing concepts, it 's time you listened to an in-depth workshop about raising your family to Christian maturity.

We want to help you fully absorb these life-changing principles, so we are offering a FREE one-hour talk on CD.

Visit www.RangerPress.com/stew.htm right now to claim your free bonus with the purchase of this book.

In this free bonus, you will discover:

- How to integrate your family into your work and ministry

- How to raise your children to Biblical maturity

- Your responsibility to raise godly children and how to fulfill it

- How to use the Bible as your final authority in all areas of life

- Practical solutions to train your children in godliness
- God's Vision for Dads

You can download the digital version, or if you prefer a hard copy CD, we can ship you a copy for $4.95 shipping & handling.

DISCOVER HOW...

You Can <u>Reduce Stress</u> and <u>Raise a Godly Family</u> by Following the Bible's Call to Blend The Areas of Family, Work and Ministry.

DOES YOUR LIFE RESEMBLE A TV DINNER?

As Christian dads, you have been taught to compartmentalize your lives. To divide your lives into areas that you can contain and effectively manage. But what happens when you seal something up and add a little heat to it?

Can you be terribly surprised when one area in your life explodes and makes a mess on all the others?

Finally, discover that the Bible does NOT teach you to compartmentalize your lives, but to carefully BLEND the areas of family, work and ministry. Don't settle for a TV dinner, make a stew! A stew that is described in Philippians 4:18 as a sweet-smelling aroma, an acceptable sacrifice, well pleasing to God.

> Integrating the God-given priorities of family, work, and ministry is the constant challenge faced by every father. In *A Father's Stew*, Stephen Beck has done us a great service by dealing biblically and practically with these issues.
>
> ~Phil Lancaster, *Patriarch Magazine*

THIS UNIQUE WORKSHOP PICKS UP WHERE THE BOOK, *A FATHER'S STEW*, ENDS.

SECRETS TO BALANCING FAMILY, WORK & MINISTRY WORKSHOP ON CD

Covering each area in greater detail, I give real-life examples from my life as well as tips on how to implement the principle of "blending the edges".

I gave this workshop to help flesh out the concepts found in the book, *A Father's Stew*.

By using real-life examples and interaction with the workshop participants, you will gain insights into implementing this strategic Biblical model in their own families. Changing old habits is extremely difficult. So I have covered in depth the nuts and bolts of changing our mindset and daily habits in order to bring about changes that will please God in our family, work and ministry.

I also understand that Dads learn in different ways, so I want to provide for you this in-depth workshop on audio so

that you can listen in the car, while exercising or doing things around the house. I want these audios to inspire you to take action with your family, take action at work and take action as you serve those around you.

> Stephen Beck doesn't just write about what it means for a father to lead his family — he's lived the life. And drawing from his experiences, he makes a passionate appeal for other men to take the steps necessary to better guide and serve their family.
>
> ~Wesley Strackbein, Vision Forum, Inc

> Direct, biblical, meaty, but yet simple and without condemnation. Wow! I can hardly wait to see what else you've written.
>
> ~Deborah Cariker, Eclectic Homeschool Online

Let me tell you what this workshop will NOT do!

- It will not change your family in 7 days.

- It will not make you fall in love with your dead-end job.

- It will not transform you into a super-Christian over night.

Discover How... 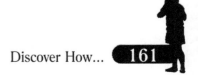 161

There is no workshop that can do that (no matter what the speaker may promise!).

But this workshop will help you to:

- See the <u>Big Picture</u>... what your life can look like when it aligns with the word of God.

- Discover **why work stinks** and what you can do about it

- Find **alternatives to working** a 9 to 5 job

- Identify **God's priorities** for fathers and how to implement them

- Learn to **live with certainty and purpose**

- Turn your **work into your calling**

- **Impact others** when you have a ton on your plate already

Steve Beck mines Scripture to paint a biblical picture of our life — that God-pleasing aroma of Christ — as a stew: a mixture of family, work and ministry. Mr. Beck's humble, down-to-earth language of this heavenly plan has challenged me to deny the worldly tendency to view my life as a TV dinner, where every aspect of my life is a separate compartment to be walled off and shut down as I move into another

> area. God never meant it to be that way, and my life is really a stew: a mixture of responsibilities, faithfulness and obedience that when balanced, blend together to create a pleasing sacrifice to God.
>
> ~Jim Bob Howard, Highlands Study Center

Christian fathers are busy! There is a lot of pressure to spend adequate time with your kids, do well in the workplace and finally, serve other believers and share the gospel. How do you do all this in a God-honoring way? This workshop on audio is designed to answer those very questions. Through Bible teaching, real-life examples and questions from the audience, I lay out a plan with specific steps to begin implementing these powerful Biblical truths.

You will receive four audio CD's that teach you in-depth ways to blend the edges of your family, work and ministry. As a result, it will be hard to tell where your family stops and your work starts. Your work stops and your ministry picks up. Your ministry leaves off and your family begins.

■ FIRST INGREDIENT: FAMILY

In an age where fathers are separated from their families for most of the day, how can you fulfill the Biblical mandate to train your children when "you sit in your house, when you walk by the way, when you lie down, and when you rise up" (Deuteronomy 6)?

Given our current culture, is it possible for you to integrate family, work and ministry in a Biblical manner? What is God's provision for raising godly children and what are your responsibilities? Hear God's vision for father as you are challenged from the Scripture to balance the areas of family, work and ministry and to blend these three ingredients to form a godly stew, a sweet smelling aroma to God.

Topics: The vision, The Bible as the ultimate authority in every area, Your responsibility in training our children in godliness, The obstacles to training your children in godliness, Some practical solutions training your children in godliness, The vision revisited

■ SECOND INGREDIENT: WORK

Has God really cursed our work so that you can only slog through the day waiting to get home where the real ministry begins? Is there more to work than meets the eye? Discover that work may not be the problem — it may be the manner in which you work!

Topics: Example of Solomon regarding our work, The average Christian's view of work, The resulting damage from a misunderstanding of work, How God views work, Practical applications for viewing work biblically

■ THIRD INGREDIENT: MINISTRY

Why is the modern church in the state that it is? Why are you so confused as to what constitutes true Biblical ministry? Why do you not see deep and lasting fruit?

We have forgotten the Great Commission! First we are to disciple our children and then we are to bring younger believers to maturity.

Included in this workshop are practical ways to teach you not merely to survive in a hostile culture, but to train battle-ready soldiers who can cross enemy lines and take captives for their Lord!

Topics: What constitutes Biblical ministry?, God's goal for ministry, God's method for maturity, Practical applications for leading men/women to maturity in Christ, The charge

■ PATRIARCHAL EXAMPLES

It is a sobering thought how many of our patriarchs in the Old Testament had disobedient children. If Eli, Samuel, David and Solomon had wayward children, what chance do we moderns have? Thankfully, the Bible shows us very clearly our responsibilities as parents and the consequences if we neglect them. Hear how you can be an immense blessing to our children by studying the parenting skills of your Old Testament forefathers.

Topics: Many of the patriarchs had rebellious children, Example of Eli, Example of Samuel, Example of David, Practical application of avoiding their mistakes

Take advantage of this Special CD Set offer by going to:

www.RangerPress.com/stewworkshop.htm

Discover How... 165

Changing Old Habits Takes Time and Your Children Are Not Getting Any Younger!

PURCHASE THIS WORKSHOP TODAY AND BEGIN IMPLEMENTING THESE POWERFUL BIBLICAL STRATEGIES BEFORE IT IS TOO LATE.

Remember, You must Work Hard Before the Concrete is Set. Don't Put Off Learning and Putting into Practice these Profound Truths.

Your Children are Depending on You.

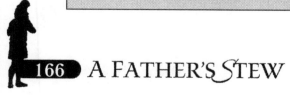

I want you to have **The Secrets to Blending Family, Work and Ministry Workshop** on CD. And I do not want affordability to be an issue. Workshops like these have steep price tags, plus the associated travel and lodging costs. I have priced this workshop very inexpensively to make sure that cost isn't an issue.

Therefore, there is no reason NOT to purchase this workshop TODAY!

The greatest problem facing Christian dads today is NOT TAKING ACTION! Do not be one of those men. The Christian world has far too many already. Order this workshop on Four CD's today and take the first step towards balancing your family, work and ministry in a biblical way.

So, take advantage of this special offer by going to:

www.RangerPress.com/stewworkshop.htm

Warmly,

Stephen Beck

P.S. If you enjoyed the book, you will love the **Secrets to Balancing Family, Work and Ministry Workshop** on CD.

PPS. Remember you have access to these Life-Changing Concepts if you go to:

www.RangerPress.com/stewworkshop.htm

Discover How... 167

Amazing! Just Insert and Listen to Discover the Secrets to Become...

 # THE CONSUMMATE MAN OF GOD

What is Required of the Man of God?

What does the Godly Man Look Like?

After all, if you are training your sons to become men who follow God and you want your daughters to marry those same type of men, you should have a good idea of how the Bible describes the consummate man of God!

Stephen Beck powerfully lays out the Biblical Vision at a Men's Retreat in the beautiful hill country of Texas. Listen and find out as Stephen encourages men to follow hard after God. He gives practical tips on training our children, showing excellence in the workplace, retooling our thinking about debt and finances and using small family businesses to further the kingdom of God.

You will receive three audio cds (about one hour each) that will transform your life.

- **THE CONSUMMATE MAN**

  The Biblical Vision of Ruling for Christ

  The Consummate Man: Psalm 112

- **WORK AND FINANCES**

  Blending our Family, Work and Ministry

  Viewing our Work Biblically

  The Biblical View of Debt and Finances

- **MINISTRY AND SERVICE**

  What is True Ministry?

  What is Necessary for the Church to Succeed in the Next 50 Years?

  Starting Small Family Businesses to Further the Kingdom of God

Above all, Stephen **fills in the gaps** and **gives the "big picture"** of living a godly life

After you listen to this tremendous Retreat CD Set, you will have the tools to raise sons and daughters who will one day rule the world.

DON'T MISS THIS POWERFUL RETREAT!

I urge you to take action today towards becoming the Consummate Man of God. Take advantage of our offer by going to:

Warmly,

Stephen Beck

P.S. Extra FREE BONUS CD! Just for trying The Consummate Man CD Set, you'll also receive our special report, Teaching Your Kids about Debt. And it's our FREE gift to you! Take advantage of our offer by going to:

www.RangerPress.com/consummate.htm

NEED THE
SECRETS

...to Balancing The Areas of Family, Work and Church, But Do Not Have Time to Read the Book?

You can now reserve your own copy of the audio version of *A Father's Stew*!

A Father's Stew:
The Biblical Integration of
Family, Work and Ministry Audio Book

You will receive four audio CD's you can play in your CD player, headset, or car.

Don't Delay! Reserve your copy TODAY at:

www.RangerPress.com/stewaudio.htm

Redeem the Time! Listen to This Fabulous Book on Your Way to Work:

www.RangerPress.com/stewaudio.htm

DYNAMIC SPEAKER WHO FILLS IN THE GAPS

...so You will Have the Tools to Raise Children to Rule and Reign for Christ, Tools to Live Debt-Free and Tools to Serve the Lord in All Areas of Life!

THE SECRETS TO BALANCING FAMILY, WORK AND MINISTRY RETREATS AND CONFERENCES
(*A Father's Stew* Retreat)

Stephen Beck is available to speak at your Retreat, Annual Conference, or Weekly Meeting.

This is not just another modern day "fluff" retreat for Christian men. It is a hard-hitting, no-nonsense approach to living the godly life, yet doing it with grace and truth.

To schedule Stephen Beck to speak at your retreat or conference, go to www.FamilyEbiz.com and click on the Contact Us button.

P.S. If you ask nicely, Stephen may even bring his potato cannons.

Printed in the USA
CPSIA information can be obtained
at www.ICGtesting.com
JSHW082205140824
68134JS00014B/446

9 781933 596549